WORLD WAR I and JEFFERSON COUNTY WEST VIRGINIA

JAMES FRANCIS HORN

THE History PRESS

Published by The History Press
Charleston, SC
www.historypress.net

First published 2017

Manufactured in the United States

ISBN 9781467119689

Library of Congress Control Number: 2017934906

Dedicated to all my friends and family who have stuck with me and supported me through all the ups and downs of my life, career and the process of working on this book.

CONTENTS

PREFACE

PLOT A, ROW 15, GRAVE 25. The year is 2012, and a student is leading a group of classmates, professors and other members of the public through the Meuse-Argonne American Cemetery. In his hand was a semester's worth of work that he was prepared to present.

The past semester had been spent in the classroom of Shepherd University's World War I history class. It was co-taught by Dr. Mark Snell and Dr. Andres Henriksson. Dr. Snell had a focus in American and military history, and Dr. Henriksson had a focus in European history. Between the two professors, the students were introduced to an expertise and an all-around eye opener that few in the United States get about the First World War, which has seemingly been forgotten in American memory. The Great War lasted more than four years and saw more than forty countries and colonies participate in it. More than 14 million people died in the war worldwide. Results of the war saw the rise of the first communist state in Russia and the emergence of the United States as a major power on the international stage. Despite how important World War I was in leading toward the rise in fascism and the Second World War and in shaping the world we have today, it is too often forgotten or overlooked in American history.

Some students in the class were given the opportunity to travel overseas to visit World War I battlefields in Belgium and France. If they wanted to receive class credit for the study abroad experience, they were to complete a single assignment: they had to find an American soldier from their hometown who was buried in one of the overseas American cemeteries from World War I, write a research paper on the soldier and present it at the soldier's grave. Months of research often made the students feel like they not only knew the experience of their soldier but also actually knew them in real life. After their research was complete and papers were written, the students boarded their flight to Paris.

The next nine days were spent traveling south along what had been known as the Western Front during the Great War. The landscape there one hundred years ago was a vast system of trenches and barbed wire that resulted in a major stalemate between the Allies and Central Powers throughout most of the war. In between the two trench systems was an area of land, small in width and covered in shell holes and mud, that was simply known as "no man's land." As the students traveled along the front, they could still see evidence of what had happened one hundred years before. French and Belgian farm fields would occasionally be interrupted by abandoned concrete bunkers. Alongside mailboxes would be piles of unexploded artillery shells that had been accidentally dug up, waiting for the government to come by and take them away. Roads were lined with British, French and occasionally German cemeteries. And when one would see a grassy meadow, it would be dimpled with one-hundred-year-old shell holes.

American monument at Montfaucon, France. *Author's collection.*

One night, the small group of students on the trip got into a discussion about all that they were seeing and how they were trying to absorb it and take it in. Eventually, the discussion went in the direction about why it is that we are fascinated by, and study, history. Some students offered up typical answers, such as "those who do not learn from history are doomed to repeat it." Others felt that they had been inspired by family or local histories that opened the door for them to want to pursue a degree in history. One student spoke up and stated that history for her was all about the "why." Everyone else in the group looked at her puzzled as she explained that one can learn almost everything about an event or period or movements in history, but what is truly fascinating is the ability to look at why it is important to the people affected by those events in history. That history is only truly important if we learn about the individual stories of the particular subject you are studying—thus "why is this important?" For the most part, this discussion was shrugged off for the rest of the trip.

The last day of the trip featured all the students giving presentations on their soldiers at the Meuse-Argonne American Cemetery, America's largest World War I cemetery and the country's largest overseas military cemetery, featuring 14,246 burials.[1] It is located on a hill in Romagne-sous-Montfaucon, France. It was the first overcast day that the students experienced the entire trip to Europe, seemingly setting the stage for them. One by one, each student led the group of professors, classmates and spectators to the grave of the selected soldier, where he or she then gave a five-minute speech. When there was one student left, he led the group toward Plot A, Row 15, Grave 25. When they arrived, all that was above ground was a white stone cross that simply read:

> *William J.H. Watters*
> *1st Lieut. 313th Inf. 79 Div.*
> *Maryland September 29, 1918*

Below this headstone was a horse racing champion, a wealthy individual, a son, a husband and a father. The student had found his "why."

That student was me, and the experiences from that trip almost five years ago have always stuck with me. I have continued to have a passion for studying the First World War ever since. Having lived in Jefferson County for the past six years, I became particularly interested in how the county was affected by the Great War. This book is not meant to change how World War I is studied or focus on the battles and campaigns of that war. Instead, this book is simply meant to help others find their "why."

Research for this book could not have been possible if not for several individuals who worked for the following organizations: Harpers Ferry National Historical Park, the Jefferson County Historical Society, the Council of Public Liberal Arts Colleges (COPLAC) and the Shepherd University Archives. Within these organizations, I need to further recognize the following individuals: the entire history staff at Shepherd University who thought highly enough of me to request I work on the COPLAC

Century America Project; Drs. Jeffery McClurken and Ellen Pearson, who through working with COPLAC assisted me with the initial research and presentation of this topic; and David Fox and Kim Biggs at Harpers Ferry National Historical Park, who gave me the freedom and support to research Storer College when the idea for this book wasn't even conceived yet. Research assistance came from the following individuals: Doug Perks (Jefferson County Historical Society), Michelle Hammer (Harpers Ferry National Historical Park) and Christy Toms (Shepherd University). The knowledge, assistance and support I received from these organizations and individuals have been incredible, inspiring and priceless. They will always have my gratitude for their assistance.

INTRODUCTION

Jefferson County, West Virginia, is located on the easternmost end of West Virginia's eastern panhandle. The county shares borders with Maryland and Virginia. The landscape features the end of the Shenandoah River, which flows into the Potomac River at Harpers Ferry. That makes Jefferson County the end of the Shenandoah Valley. The eastern border of the county features the Blue Ridge Mountains, and most of the county is made up of rolling hills. The combination of mountains, waterways and hills makes for a spectacular landscape that attracts hundreds of thousands of visitors every year. But below the surface of this beautiful landscape is a rich history that makes Jefferson County one of the most important regions in American history.

Jefferson County features the oldest town in West Virginia in Shepherdstown, which began to be settled 130 years before West Virginia separated from Virginia.[2] Along the banks of the Potomac and Shenandoah Rivers, the United States of America's first president, George Washington, would establish one of the nation's first arsenals and armories at Harpers Ferry, which put Jefferson County at the forefront of the American industrial age. And just to the south of his armory, George Washington's brother Charles established what would become the county seat in the town of Charles Town. As the county's population and production grew, so did its importance and connection to the rest of the world.

The county gained a direct connection to the nation's capital, Washington D.C., when the Chesapeake and Ohio (C&O) Canal was built along the

Potomac River. This revolutionized the amount of time it took for citizens to travel and transport goods along the sixty-mile trip to the District of Columbia. Just a year after the arrival of the C&O Canal, a more modern piece of technology arrived in the form of railroads. The Baltimore and Ohio (B&O) Railroad brought a direct connection to the port city of Baltimore. And not long after the B&O Railroad arrived, another railroad would make its appearance in the Winchester and Potomac Railroad. This line went from the Shenandoah Valley city of Winchester north to Harpers Ferry, where it met the B&O Railroad. With these developments, Jefferson County became an industrial and transportation hub of the United States. Settlement grew in the county, and production soared, creating a period of profit and prosperity for the citizens who lived there. This prosperity was not to last, however.

Jefferson County became the focal point for one of the most dramatic stories in American history. In 1859, an abolitionist by the name of John Brown attacked the arsenal and armory at Harpers Ferry in an attempt to acquire weapons for a slave revolt. Brown failed and was captured, along with most of his men being killed or captured. After his capture, the world's eyes were fixated as he was moved just down the road to the county seat at Charles Town. There Brown, and seemingly the entire institution of slavery, was put on trial, accused of murder, treason and inciting slave rebellion. The entire country was split on what Brown had done and his trial. At the end of it, however, the jury of Jefferson County citizens found Brown guilty on all three counts, and he was hanged just a month later. The events in Jefferson County in 1859 had effectively split the nation and set up the tension to come in the 1860 election.

After the fallout from Abraham Lincoln's election in 1860, many Southern states feared for the future of slavery in their states and began to secede from the Union. In April 1861, Virginia made the decision to leave the Union and join these states in creating the Confederate States of America. Jefferson County, still part of Virginia at this time, found itself on the front lines of the war, with enemy territory being right across the Potomac River. Almost immediately after Virginia left the Union, Jefferson County felt the effects of war. American soldiers burned the arsenal and armory at Harpers Ferry and burned the B&O Railroad bridge, destroying the industrial center of the county and cutting its economic ties to port cities. With destruction immediately hitting Jefferson County, many citizens lost their jobs and left, and others fled looking to avoid being on the front lines of war. These actions drastically drained the once prosperous county of a workforce.

The four-year Civil War that followed had drastic effects on the future of Jefferson County. The county found itself right in the path of Southern armies moving north to invade Maryland and Pennsylvania, as well as their route back south. It also became the staging point for Northern armies to attempt to capture the Shenandoah Valley. The bloodiest battle in what is now West Virginia was fought just outside Shepherdstown, and the largest surrender of United States forces (until World War II) occurred at Harpers Ferry. The famous courthouse where John Brown had been put on trial in Charles Town was shelled by artillery, shot at by infantry and used for stables, leaving the once beautiful building in shambles. In the midst of all this destruction, however, Jefferson County did see some creation.

When Virginia left the Union, many of the western counties of Virginia had felt that they were dragged into the wrong side of the conflict. In Wheeling, Virginia, delegates from these counties met several times to discuss breaking off from their mother state. In 1863, Congress and citizens of these western counties approved the creation of the new state of West Virginia. With this separation came the three counties that make up the tip of the Eastern Panhandle of West Virginia: Morgan, Berkeley and Jefferson Counties. These counties had been split on the issue of rejoining the Union, but through political maneuvering, they largely voted to become part of the state of West Virginia. Despite rejoining the Union, Jefferson County found no relief from the front lines of war, as it now shared what Southerners believed was an international border with Virginia at the crest of the Blue Ridge Mountains to the east and the southern border of the county. After another nearly two more years of war, Jefferson County finally found peace when the Southern armies surrendered, bringing an end to the conflict. But by the end of the Civil War, Jefferson County had been nearly destroyed, and its citizens were left to pick up the pieces and attempt to rebuild.

Fifty years later, in the early twentieth century, Jefferson County still hadn't fully recovered from the war. Although life moved on, some areas of the county were still struggling to regain what they had before the Civil War. It was during this period that America once again found itself in a time of war. Jefferson County, however, found a new role for itself from what it had half a century before. Instead of being on the front lines, the war was occurring an ocean away, and Jefferson County would be a part of the homefront. The county and its citizens rose to the challenge and gave their all in support of the United States' role in the First World War. Red Cross members raised money for supplies and support of American soldiers, the county's large agricultural community moved into action to produce food during rationing and the county felt the devastation of the Spanish influenza that swept across the country. Of course, many young men found themselves in combat roles, and the local draft board saw to it that Jefferson County did its part. West Virginia as a whole mustered more than 58,000 men for active duty service during the Great War.[3] Of that number, more than 530 came directly from Jefferson County, plus more than 300 soldiers came from college institutions within the county.[4]

The citizens of Jefferson County gave everything in support of their country in a time of war. These are their stories.

Chapter 1

SHEPHERDSTOWN

In 1734, a man by the name of Thomas Shepherd purchased land grants for an area on the south banks of the Potomac River along a small stream called Falling Spring Branch. Shepherd settled the land, and soon others followed, establishing the town of Mecklenburg. The stream would later become known as Town Run, as it flowed right through the center of town. Years after Thomas Shepherd's death, the town renamed itself Shepherdstown, after its founder. This is the oldest town in modern-day West Virginia.

Shepherdstown is no stranger to war. In 1775, George Washington made a call for Virginia riflemen to join him in New England around the start of the American Revolution. An entire company of riflemen was formed in Shepherdstown and then made the famous Beeline March, fulfilling its patriotic duty. In 1862, in the midst of the American Civil War, Shepherdstown saw the more horrific side of war. In September of that year, the Union Army of the Potomac and the Confederate Army of Northern Virginia met on the opposite side of the Potomac River from Shepherdstown, outside Sharpsburg, Maryland. There the two armies fought the Battle of Antietam, which became the single bloodiest day in American history. More than twenty-two thousand men were killed, wounded or went missing during this battle.[5] As a result, a steady stream of wounded men entered Shepherdstown, and the citizens went into action, with every home, church, public building and small shed being converted into makeshift hospitals. Just two days later, parts of the two armies met again on the outskirts of town,

Historic view of German Street in Shepherdstown. 1912. *Shepherd University Archives.*

and the Battle of Shepherdstown became the bloodiest battle to occur within what is today the state of West Virginia.

Shepherdstown survived the Civil War but had much rebuilding to do after the war was over. By the turn of the century, shops were once again lining German Street (the main street in town), a railroad line came through town and stretched across the Potomac River and the town had become a popular tourist spot for people from large cities who admired its quaintness and the beautiful landscape that surrounded it. With a sense of normalcy returning to Shepherdstown nearly fifty years later, the memories of the Civil War might have been completely forgotten had it not been for surviving veterans, bloodstains on the floors of buildings that had been used as hospitals and the Confederate burials in Elmwood Cemetery.

War was the last thing on anyone's mind in 1914, which made for a surprise when word reached across the ocean in August that several European nations had declared war on one another. On August 6, readers of the *Shepherdstown Register* opened the town newspaper to find an article grimly titled, "War":

> *What may be the greatest war this world has ever known has been started in Europe. For years the great European nations have been arming themselves for what seemed to them to be an inevitable conflict, and now the*

> *grim dogs of war have all been let loose. The cause of the outburst seems comparatively trifling to bring about so terrible a war. A few weeks ago the crown prince of Austria and his wife were assassinated by members of a secret political order in* [Serbia].[6]

In August 1914, the powers in Europe began declaring war on one another, and through a system of entangling alliances, other countries were dragged into the conflict one by one. At the beginning, no one around the world really knew what to expect regarding the outcome of the war. The powers that entered the conflict felt that they had a divine power looking out for their interests, one that would lead them to victory. For the people of Shepherdstown, and much of the rest of the United States, the conflict was an ocean away, forcing them to watch in horror as the Great War became bloodier and larger in scale. Although not yet in the war, effects from the world war were felt at home by Shepherdstown citizens. The products being manufactured and grown in nearby areas and making their way to Shepherdstown to board trains or the canal found themselves backed up because "the war in Europe [had] caused an almost entire cessation of shipping and as a consequence imports to the United States [had] fallen off so greatly that revenues are seriously reduced."[7]

Shepherdstown residents sat and watched, wondering what America's role in this world war would be. When it was reported that President Wilson had meetings with the leaders of France, which wanted to borrow large sums of money to get the United States involved in the war, and he had denied this proposal, many in Shepherdstown supported his decision. One reporter stated:

> *It will cause our government to retain the respect of all the belligerents and they will naturally look to us when the time for mediating comes; and if money cannot be obtained from outside sources the war is going to have to be shortened. We have a great President in the White House.*[8]

The president's decision to remain neutral in the world war was so popular in Shepherdstown that when Woodrow Wilson made a request to the American people in October of that year to hold a day of prayer for peace, Shepherdstown enthusiastically answered. Shepherdstown citizens met on the campus of Shepherd College, where in the Shepherd College Hall they came together as one congregation to pray for peace. The *Shepherdstown Register* described the event:

A chapel service being held in the Shepherd College auditorium, located in Knutti Hall. 1913. *Shepherd University Archives.*

> *Fervent prayers were offered during the service by Rev. C. Sydenstricker, of the M.E. Church South; Rev. Dr. Charles Ghiselin, of the Presbyterian Church; and Rev. William Rogers, of the Methodist Church. The music was in charge of Prof. J.D. Muldoon, and was led by a large choir of local singers, who rendered with the fine effect a special anthem. The congregational singing was particularly good, hymns appropriate to the occasion being sung….A collection was taken for the benefit of the Red Cross Society, and the sum of fifty dollars was contributed. The meeting was one that will long be remembered by those who were privileged to be present.*[9]

Although the war was an ocean away, there was one Shepherdstown resident who experienced the start of the Great War firsthand. Professor John N. Ware, whose parents still lived in Shepherdstown, was living in Paris doing research when the war broke out. That August, as France was plunged into war, he wrote home to his parents:

> *I will not leave Paris until the very last minute, as all Americans are perfectly safe, and if they have somewhere to stay and enough money for their needs, it would be crazy to leave at this epoch making hour….Just one day was there any rioting, when several German-owned shops were wrecked by hoodlums. But this was repressed so sternly, some three hundred rioters being imprisoned as seditious subjects (a serious charge in these times) that it has not occurred again….I went down to see some of my German friends off on the last train out; and the scenes at the depot that night were simply indescribable, for there was a perfect stampede to get away before the bars*

> *were put up, that cut Germans and Austrians off from their countries. Those who could not get away have been sent to some town in the west of France, where they will be kept under watch.*[10]

Mr. Ware's letter at the outset of the war was read with much interest by the residents of Shepherdstown, who were anxiously waiting to hear news of the European war. It is likely that the older residents of Shepherdstown, who had experienced what it was like at the beginning of the Civil War, could draw some parallels between Mr. Ware's experiences in Paris and what they had gone through more than fifty years earlier.

John Ware was one of thousands of Americans who found themselves in Europe when the war started. The tone of his letter seems rather relaxed, as he believed that he was out of any sort of combat area and that Paris was a safe city for any American to be in. His tone would change in just a few weeks when the German army, as part of its "Schlieffen Plan" (the German mobilization plan in the event that the country was to get into a war with France) went into action. The fast-moving German war machine soon found its armies approaching the French capital at alarming speeds. With the city in danger, Americans scrambled to leave Paris and eventually the country as a whole. Mr. Ware reportedly boarded the last train out of the city at this time, and while he saw no fighting, he did witness the many troops of the French army mobilizing to deal with the threat. Upon his return to the United States with his wife, he immediately went to his parents' home in Shepherdstown, where he recounted his experiences for the *Shepherdstown Register*:[11]

> *War came on us in Paris so quickly that we scarcely realized that it was imminent. There were some eleven Germans in our pension, one of them an officer on leave, and from day to day they went to the German consulate for advice. Things were not so serious as to make the consulate advise Germans to leave Paris….*[T]*he next day notices were posted, ordering all German and Austrian subjects to be out by ten that night; all who were found later would be sent to detention camps in the west of France….Mobilization went on quietly, and one by one the classes went out, a day at a time. In our pension the son went on the second day, the son-in-law on the fourth, the concierge on the seventh and three boarders at the various time; each time with no heroics or hysteria, also no singing or cheering. It was too serious a business….About the 26th of August, when the spectacular German advance on Paris was beginning, news vendors were not allowed to utter a*

> *sound, and it was uncanny to see these old men, boys, women, and children, running silently down the streets waving their papers like wings.*[12]

Mr. Ware left France right before the First Battle of the Marne was fought. Likely the massive increase of troops he saw in Paris just prior to his departure was part of the famous "Taxi Cab Army," where French soldiers were rushed to the front from Paris using the city's taxi cabs, arriving just in time to save the French capital. After John Ware returned home from Europe, Shepherdstown's link to the European war was seemingly cut, and little attention was paid to the conflict. Occasional articles appeared talking about the changing styles of warfare and the creation of a massive line of trenches in eastern France and western Belgium, as well as each time a new nation entered the fray. But most of all, Americans just hoped for peace in Europe before their nation was dragged into the conflict.

Perhaps what caught the eyes of Shepherdstown's population the most was news of the Belgian refugee crisis. In Germany's plan at the start of the war, a quick movement of soldiers was needed to take out Paris. The plan called for the quickest route to be taken to achieve this: through the small country of Belgium. When Belgium refused to allow the German military access through its country, it was quickly dragged into war. The much larger German army made quick work of getting through the country. This action dragged Britain into the Great War, as it claimed it was now fighting for Belgian neutrality and sovereignty. When battle lines were drawn, and as hostile waters surrounded Europe, it became increasingly difficult for the Central Powers to get any goods or information sent to the United States. England, on the other hand, had little issue doing this, so the United States became flooded with British propaganda on the atrocities of the German state, in particular the atrocities that Germany was inflicting on the Belgian people. Americans' heads were being filled with images of Belgian children starving in the streets and innocent civilians being executed daily. While there were atrocities committed in Belgium, they were rather minor in comparison to what Britain was claiming. Nonetheless, Shepherdstown citizens looked to open their hearts to help those suffering in Belgium. An ad in January 1915 told the people of Shepherdstown that "arrangements [were] made for sending parcel post packages from rural districts" and that Shepherdstown citizens could help "aid the stricken little sister of the world."[13]

Despite the large imports of British propaganda, feelings toward the war not only in America but especially in Shepherdstown were relatively neutral. Shepherdstown, like most of the Shenandoah Valley of West Virginia and

Going by several different names, today the structure known simply as the "Yellow House" is considered the oldest standing house in Shepherdstown. 1915. *Shepherd University Archives.*

Virginia, had a strong German influence going back to the days when the valley was first settled. It is likely that this influence helped offset the British propaganda. However, in May 1915, this feeling of neutrality would be put to the test. It had long been known that German submarines were conducting a system of unrestricted warfare, meaning that they would attack any vessel in their war zone without warning. This had long troubled many Americans since it violated the American value of "Freedom of the Seas," which could find its roots dating back to George Washington. On May 7, 1915, German submarines sank a vessel traveling from the United States to Great Britain called the *Lusitania.* The ship had a crew of about 800 men and more than 1,200 passengers on board, with nearly 200 of them being American. More than 1,200 people lost their lives in the attack. The *Shepherdstown Register* had this to say on the attack:

> *The Lusitania was almost at its journey's end when a German submarine suddenly appeared, and without warning of any sort of giving the doomed voyagers a chance for their lives, fired a torpedo that struck the ship squarely and tore a great hole in its side. As the huge vessel reeled and settled in the water from the shock of the explosion, the murderous crew of the submarine sent two more torpedoes crashing into its sides. In a few moments the ship*

> *went to the bottom carrying most of the passengers and crew with it.... The whole world is aghast at the wicked cruelty and savage, murderous spirit of the Germans that caused such wanton destruction of innocent and harmless people.... This wicked and unpardonable crime against humanity and civilization is the natural result of the war spirit that has been fostered as a national characteristic by the Germans for the past forty years. They have become a brutal and savage people, without regard for human life or human rights.*[14]

The world watched with anticipation after the *Lusitania* was sunk to see if America was going to be dragged into the world war, but tensions settled, keeping the United States at peace. Germany agreed to end its unrestricted submarine warfare in order to ease the tensions. But the *Lusitania* incident made clear to Shepherdstown residents, and small towns all across the United States, that if America was to ever enter the world war, it would likely not join the Central Powers.

Despite the troubling news abroad, Shepherdstown also found some time for celebration in 1915. Long had there been a push to find a way to honor James Rumsey in the town. Rumsey is credited by many for having invented the steamboat. In 1785, Rumsey went to the banks of the Potomac River just below the bluffs of Shepherdstown and tested out his invention. Although the boat had its problems, it was considered a major milestone in working toward making ships independent from relying on wind power. In 1915, work had been completed on a large stone pillar monument just outside the town, overlooking the Potomac River, where it still exists today. The monument was celebrated by many upon its completion. A student of Shepherd College described the accomplishment:

> *The column is intended to be a pure Ionic design, the prototypes of which are found on the shores of Asia Minor, built in the fourth century, B.C. It is Particularly fitting that the Ionic order be used to express James Rumsey's invention. The Ionians were people of the sea, and through them the graceful Ionic column was brought from the East into Greece.... To further symbolize the greatness and wide-spread results of the invention, a massive granite globe surmounts the column. The continents are carved in high relief. The proportion and form of the memorial are intended to make it a landmark and dominant feature.*[15]

As the months rolled by, less and less focus was being put on the war that was an ocean away. The year 1916 saw an election year of great importance. Many residents of Shepherdstown put an emphasis on finding candidates for local elections who supported prohibition. On a national level, Woodrow Wilson was running for reelection as president of the United States against Republican Charles E. Hughes. Wilson ran on the slogan "He kept us out of war," which many Americans felt wasn't an easy task given the state of global affairs. Wilson won his reelection bid, but events overseas were putting the United States on a collision course toward war nonetheless.

In 1917, the state of the war was looking good for Germany and its Central Powers allies. Its opponent to the east, Russia, was falling out of the war as Vladimir Lenin's Communist revolution took over the country. With Russia out of the picture, Germany had millions of troops free to move toward the western front to take on Britain and France. With what appeared to be a sure victory in the world war within grasp, Germany no longer felt the need to tiptoe around the United States. Once again German submarines moved to a policy of unrestricted warfare. At the same time this occurred, a document came to light called the "Zimmerman Telegram," a message sent from Germany to Mexico imploring the Mexican government to declare war on the United States in the event that the American government decided to declare war on Germany. Now Germany was not only violating the freedom of the seas but also hemispheric separation, a second pillar of American foreign policy.

With Germany blatantly violating American policies, Woodrow Wilson felt he had no choice. On April 2, 1917, just one month after being inaugurated into his second term of office after running on a noninterventionist slogan, Wilson made a speech to Congress imploring it to declare war on Germany. Just four days later, Congress would oblige, and the United States was plunged into the chaos of the First World War. The country did not have much preparation for a war already in place, so almost immediately an emphasis was placed on small farming communities, such as Shepherdstown, to work on food production. The governor of West Virginia, John J. Cornwell, greeted the people of Shepherdstown on the morning of April 12, extolling to them the importance of farming production:

> *May I suggest that no greater public service can be rendered at this time than in calling attention of the people, especially those who reside in villages and small towns, to the importance of larger agricultural productions, particularly that of utilizing every inch of available garden space in planting and producing potatoes and other vegetables.*[16]

Shepherdstown responded to the governor's wishes with great enthusiasm. Almost every free spot of land in town was converted into a liberty garden, farm hands went to great lengths to put in extra hours of work and daily propaganda was printed in support of the local farmers. In the spring of 1918, farmers who had been drafted and were in training would even be given special treatment to return home in order to help with the planting season. The war department released a statement noting that "furloughs granted under such order will be for short periods only, at seeding and harvesting time. Furloughs may be denied, however, if it is found they would seriously interfere with the training of the men wanted."[17] The community of Shepherdstown even came together to make sure that neighbors were getting the most out of their liberty gardens to help manage life under rationing. Recipes were released on different foods involving potatoes, such as this one for potato war bread:

> *Heat milk to boiling point, then cool to luke-warm. Bake or boil potatoes, then mash or put through ricer. Dissolve yeast cake in the milk. Make a sponge as follows: mix milk, yeast cake, salt, sugar, all the mashed or riced potatoes and one third of the flour. Beat well, let stand over night to rise. In the morning add balance of flour—let rise again until double in the bulk, then mold into a loaf; let rise again to double in bulk, then bake 40 minutes in a moderate oven. A little more flour will be required if potatoes are not mealy.*[18]

Then there was this one for potato doughnuts:

> *Mix sugar, spices, salt and shortening. Add well-beaten egg and milk. Beat well and add flour and baking powder which have been shifted together. Mold on board and roll to half in chick, cut with doughnut cutter and fry in deep fat.*[19]

In an effort to generate support for the war, a wave of patriotism swept over Shepherdstown. Not long after America entered the war, German Street (the main road through Shepherdstown) was renamed as Main Street to show support for America's declaration of war.[20] The Shepherdstown Opera House did its part to spread the patriotic spirit by showing various films that related to the war or celebrated the history of the United States. In July and August 1918, the opera house showed *Pershing's Crusaders*, which was described thus: "Uncle Sam photographed it. Uncle Sam will be pleased if you see it." The opera house held the distinct honor of being the first venue in West Virginia to be able to present the film.[21]

The need for such a patriotic spirt in Shepherdstown, as well as the rest of the country, was seen in the attempt to raise money for the government to be able to fight the war. The most common way to raise this money was through the purchase of liberty bonds, for which Shepherdstown certainly did its part. The United States government at the start of the war was looking to raise $5 billion in bonds. Bonds could be purchased in increments from $50 to $100,000, with an interest rate of 3.5 percent. This ensured that "the smallest investor may be able to purchase, as well as the rich." The Jefferson Security Bank was the main location where Shepherdstown residents, as well as other Jefferson County residents, could purchase these bonds.[22] By April 1918, Shepherdstown was already going "over the top" with the apportionment set out for the town to reach in buying liberty bonds. The town's apportionment for the Third Liberty Loan was $45,300, which was quickly exceeded. The town received a flag from the secretary of the treasury as a prize for its donation. Despite this success, the *Shepherdstown Register* still let readers know that "every person in the community who can do so is urged to buy a bond, whether it be for a large or small amount, and thus show our loyalty and our progressiveness."[23]

To further increase liberty bond sales, President Woodrow Wilson declared April 26, 1918, to be Liberty Day. This was a way to keep the patriotic fervor going more than a year after war had been declared. Shepherdstown participated in this declaration with a patriotic parade, and all automobiles were decorated with the stars and stripes. The day also provided more opportunities to purchase liberty bonds, as well as war savings stamps.[24] The mayor of Shepherdstown, J.L. Waldeck, released a statement in support of Liberty Day:

> *For one hundred and forty years the people of the United States have enjoyed freedom as a nation under our present form of government. We have prospered and grown in numbers, wealth and power as no other nation has ever grown. Today the serpent of autocracy has coiled and is now ready to strike the most vital principles of free government everywhere.... [W]e are called to purchase liberty bonds without stint or limit. Now therefore I, J.L. Waldeck, Mayor of Shepherdstown, do by this proclamation designate and set apart April 26, 1918, as Liberty Day to be observed as President Wilson requests.*[25]

Also in April 1918, word had spread that a train was passing through town that was carrying soldiers. With Shepherdstown's citizens wanting to show their patriotism, a rather interesting event unfolded:

> *Last Thursday evening word got around that a train load of soldiers from one of the southern camps would pass through Shepherdstown at 5 30 o'clock....* [F]*olks thought that this would be a good chance to at least get a glimpse of the soldiers as they went north on their way to France. The girls of the town put on their prettiest frocks and their sweetest smiles and hurried to the stations, resolved to cheer the hearts of the soldier boys, if only for a brief space. Presently the train whistled, and the girls lined up on the station platform looking too sweet and pretty for words. Then the train came along at about forty miles an hour, but not a soldier was to be seen, for the car windows were opaque with mist and snow and the girls couldn't see in and the boys couldn't see out. The smiles of tenderness turned into sickly grins as the girls gazed at the receding rear end of the train—and the soldiers don't know yet how much they missed at Shepherdstown.*[26]

With its rise in patriotism and support for the war effort, Shepherdstown also saw a rise in fear. Shepherdstown citizens looked at their railroad bridge and the C&O Canal across the river from them as likely targets of German spies and saboteurs. Certainly, the canal and various bridges and railroads had been targets all throughout the Civil War, and this rested in the back of the minds of some. But these forms of transportation were also vital to America's mobilization efforts and supply movement, so if saboteurs did reside in the United States, why wouldn't these be targets? To see to the possible security threat, put the minds of townspeople at ease and likely also work as a recruitment tool, Maryland National Guard troops were stationed by the railroad bridge. The *Shepherdstown Register* reported, "The soldiers guarding the bridge of the Norfolk & Western Railway at Shepherdstown are using a freight car, that has been set on a side track as headquarters and living apartments. A telephone has been installed, with a private wire to the local exchange."[27] In order to keep the C&O Canal operational during the war, there was an effort made by the Railroad Administration to get the government to "assume the operation and improvement of the canal."[28] By this time, the C&O Canal was showing that it couldn't stand up to the task at hand to provide ample transportation of goods in a time of war. The canal was largely in need of repairs in some areas, and in some areas, the canal had a tunnel that was not wide enough for boats to pass alongside each other, forcing long lines of traffic. With reports of the canal failing to provide sufficient transportation, many people in Shepherdstown likely found comfort in the canal across the river from them not being attacked.

Perhaps Shepherdstown's greatest contribution to the war effort was its enthusiastic participation and support of the American Red Cross. The Red Cross had an important role in the war effort. Red Cross chapters often raised money for the war effort, received donations of needed war matériel, stitched clothes for soldiers or even sent care packages to soldiers to keep morale up. America's entry into the First World War saw a spike in Red Cross members. By January 1918, the Jefferson County chapter of the Red Cross had grown to roughly 2,000 members.[29] Shepherdstown's Red Cross membership was at 535 members, an increase of 322 from the original 213 members.[30] It was clear that Shepherdstown was going to do its part for the Red Cross.

The chapter engaged in various activities to support the war effort. In the spring of 1918, the Jefferson County Red Cross sold eggs, raising $294.00 for the war effort—$54.45 of this came from the Shepherdstown chapter.[31] In the month of April 1918, the Shepherdstown Red Cross reported the following numbers for donated items to the war: 40 muslin hospital shirts, 5 canton flannel hospital shirts, 5 outing hospital shirts, 24 suit pajamas, 2 pairs of bed socks, 2 pairs of bandaged foot socks, 9 sweaters, 8 pairs of socks, 1 helmet and 1,400 gauge compresses.[32] The Jefferson County Red Cross continued the success through the war, reporting that during the summer it donated the following items: 2,649 garments, 12,050 surgical dressings, 505 comfort kits, 505 housewives (sewing kits), 400 pairs of socks and 255 sweaters.[33] The Red Cross also had a heavy presence at the Charles Town Horse Show in August 1918. The show worked out that all proceeds from the event, other than the entrance fee, would be donated to support the Red Cross's war effort. Shepherdstown ran a booth where donated items would be auctioned off to bidders. The items included pigs, ponies and chickens.[34]

All of the Red Cross's effort did not go unnoticed by the soldiers serving their country. When the soldiers received Christmas boxes, many wrote back home to tell how much they appreciated the gift. One soldier, Ernest B. Hamrick, wrote to the Shepherdstown Red Cross:

> *I wish to express my hearty appreciation and thanks for your kind remembrance. It surely did bring joy and cheer to know that we are remembered by the folks in our home town, and I wish to thank you individually and as an organization. You are doing splendid work.*[35]

Another soldier, Harry H. Walper, received a box of cookies and felt that he had to express his gratitude to the Shepherdstown Red Cross for the gift:

> *I am very, very much indebted to you all for the delicious box of sugar cookies which, you so thoughtfully and kindly sent to me over here, and which have just been received. The package arrived in excellent condition, and the cookies are the best I have ever eaten, all for which I am greatly thankful.... The good work of the Red Cross can be noticed everywhere, and taken together with the Y.M.C.A., they are doing an unlimited amount of good for our boys.*[36]

While Shepherdstown was hard at work at home helping with the war effort, several of its sons either enlisted or were drafted to do their part on the front lines of the war. Many of these soldiers wrote home and had their letters printed in the *Shepherdstown Register* so the public could read about their adventures, hardships and uplifting stories of patriotism and heroism. While not all the soldiers made it overseas before the armistice was signed in November 1918, those who did make it to France were closely watched from home by their friends, family and neighbors who looked for news of their well-being. Soldiers had to face many dangers from training accidents to disease spreading around camps, German U-boats that would target transport ships and combat itself—all causing heartaches for mothers and other loved ones at home.

One soldier who saw a lot of action in the military was Cleon S. Osbourn, who was from Shenandoah Junction, not far outside Shepherdstown. Cleon was part of the Sixth Field Artillery in the First Division of the American Expeditionary Forces (AEF). Being in the First Division meant that Cleon was among the first Americans to see any action at the front in the Great War. In March 1918, Cleon reached the rank of lieutenant and wrote home of his experiences:

> *Since the first of the month the Germans have been a little more active, but we have hushed them up in good shape every time so far. The French in written orders and otherwise have highly commended the U.S. boys, who have been showing wonderful spirit in every way....* [W]*e are poking a lot of hot lead and steel over into the Germans. Last night I noticed the sound of the shells outside of the noise of the shots themselves. You can hear them going over like the rushing of mighty waters, and in the night when the great line of guns goes off, the whole heavens are lighted up.*[37]

Cleon continued to keep in touch with his family, sending them many letters and packages to keep them at ease. In one package, he sent home a Paris copy of the *New York Herald*, and he described how amazed he was that the "brave men from Dixie land and from Yankee towns" got along so well in the trenches. When Lieutenant Osbourn reflected on the possibilities of death, he said, "I am still counting as much as ever, of course, on getting back to the old U.S., but if I do not, you know that I will give all cheerfully. If others must, why shouldn't I?"[38] In May 1918, the First Division was preparing for an attack on the French town of Cantigny. The town was held by Germans and would be the first offensive from any American units in the war. As the division was gearing up for this attack, Lieutenant Osbourn wrote home, giving a glimpse into what he was thinking about:

> *Today has been filled with thoughts of mother and all her wonderful love....My thoughts and prayers have been with you all day, and of course I have been filled, heart and soul, with appreciation of all your wonderful love. Everything goes well here so far. It has been quieter than I expected to find it, but it livens a little at times....The French are great and very appreciative of America's help....It is good to be with the French in this great struggle, and we all feel honored to be here.*[39]

The *Shepherdstown Register*, upon printing his many letters, described Cleon as a loving son and heroic soldier. Despite being in the midst of offensives in France, Lieutenant Osbourn always found time to write home. Once he apologized for the rushed nature of his previous letter, which was due to being in the midst of a gas attack that had lasted for forty-five hours continuously, but he and his battery came out unharmed. This is how Cleon described the actual battle for Cantigny:

> *Our infantry boys on a certain second all rose up over the top of the front line trench, and in an unbroken line marched forward over the top of a German hill, and carried both hill and village (Cantigny) and then established a new forward line. Soon afterward came gang after gang of German prisoners, being marched along by our infantry boys. Four big groups of them went by our battery. I am enclosing a mark which lieutenant Evans of our battery traded a franc for....But no sooner had we established the new line than here came the German counter attacks. Eight times they came, twice with tanks, but each time they were hurled back....[N]ow things have settled down again, with our boys in full possession of the new field. It has been*

> *an inspiration for all of us, and if Uncle Sam hurries on over with the five million that Billy Taft and Teddy Roosevelt want, it will not take long to bring on the right end.*[40]

Lieutenant Osbourn continued to serve on the front lines with the First Division until the end of July 1918. At the end of this month, his parents looked out their front door and saw a soldier approaching their doorstep. It was Cleon, sent back to the United States without informing his parents, who were so surprised that they thought it was a ghost approaching their house. Cleon was described as looking well, but he also showed signs "that he [had] been through tremendous experience." The reunion with his family was short-lived, as Cleon was soon sent to New York to help with the training of new recruits.[41] Not long after Lieutenant Osbourn returned to the United States, it was made public that he was being cited for gallantry in action. Cleon's commanding officer, Lieutenant Colonel Parker, had this to say in the citation:

> *The Regimental Commander cites to the regiments the fine conduct and performance of the commanding officer and the men of the advance battery position of F Battery during the night of June 25–26. These men, under the direction of Lieutenant Osbourn, fought a fire started by German incendiary shells near the battery position in Coullemelle. Although subjected to harassing fire by German 77mm. guns and in danger of being hit by exploding 75mm. shells and machine gun bullets, stored in the building, they saved most of the ammunition and after a two hour struggle brought the fire under control.*[42]

Cleon would spend the rest of the war training soldiers, with the war ending while he was in Alabama training members of the Twenty-Sixth Field Artillery waiting for orders to return to France.[43]

R.D. Shipley was another Shepherdstown boy serving overseas. Shipley was serving in the First Division of the Ordnance Mobile Repair Shops. His brother, Elkins, was also serving with the AEF in France, making the Shipley family very nervous for their sons. R.D. wrote home often to keep in touch. This is how he described the voyage to Europe:

> *Father, that lonesome voyage across the angry seas was very bad, for we had stormy weather most all the way, and I was so seasick I almost died. Each and every day I would look back with troubled eyes in the direction of the*

old U.S.A., for, believe me, there is no place on earth that can compete with dear old U.S.A., for that's where I long to be. France is very beautiful, what part I have seen, but the climate where we are stationed is very damp and cold. Elkins and I have very bad colds but are getting better now.[44]

One of Corporal Shipley's favorite things while he was overseas was receiving letters from home. He so enjoyed this that he scolded his mother in one letter for her seeming lack of participation in this, saying, "What in the world has become of you? Are you lost, strayed or stolen? I have been in France over two months and the thing I will appreciate is a letter from home."[45] As time moved on, R.D. Shipley worked hard in France, carefully taking in all the experiences abroad. This is how he described Memorial Day in France:

Today is Memorial Day in the United States as well as in France. They had a great time over here. There are a good many Americans and aviators laid to rest here beneath the sod of beautiful France, only about a mile from where I am stationed, and the French and Americans decorated their graves with wreaths of flowers of the most beautiful sort. American and French aviators flew over the graves and dropped flowers upon them as they passed. All who were there shed tears, and the French people wept over the American graves as they did over those of their own soldiers. We are very busy over here now. The great drive is starting and I am where I can hear and see it all.[46]

Throughout their experiences, the Shipley brothers sent many souvenirs home to their parents that they found on the battlefields. This included a German leather belt, a German cap, bullets and shell fragments. The pieces were put on display in the window of Owen's drugstore in Shepherdstown.[47] R.D. was very proud of his service and wrote to his brother about his experiences in the fall of 1918:

I am where they are falling the thickest, and I am proud of it. The more excitement, the better I like it, and believe me we have some of it. I have seen dead Germans in this present drive ten and twelve deep. The Yanks boys know how to do the work. Do you remember back in school when we were studying history how those old fellows pulled off their great tricks? Well, the Yankees are doing the same stunts and they cannot be equaled.[48]

R.D. Shipley went on to survive the final push the U.S. forces made to help end the Great War and saw the war to the end.

One of the soldiers from Shepherdstown who was most closely followed was William B. Snyder. Snyder's father was the editor of the *Shepherdstown Register* during the First World War, and when his son joined the American military, he was determined to share his son's experiences with his readers. Through William's eyes, many Shepherdstown citizens began to understand the firsthand experiences of the war. "Bill" was a member of the Second Motor Mechanic Regiment and found himself traveling all over the country to train for the war. He started in New Orleans and then went to Alabama; Augusta, Georgia; and eventually New Jersey. While stationed in New Jersey, awaiting to go "Over There," William Snyder was promoted to the rank of sergeant.[49] When Bill did eventually make it overseas, he sent a simple message to his father: "Have arrived safely overseas." It was reported that this lifted a heavy weight from his father's heart, who was worried for Bill's safety in crossing the Atlantic for fear of German U-boats.[50] As Sergeant Snyder continued his work in France, he regularly wrote home to tell his father of the good work he was doing and of his observations of life in wartime France, like how the war bread tasted more like cake or how appreciative the French people were for the job the Americans were doing. In one of his letters, Bill talked about the death of Quentin Roosevelt, son of Theodore Roosevelt:

> *Today comes the confirmation of the death of Quentin Roosevelt, and every man in this camp feels deeply the loss of this splendid fellow. He was a frequent visitor here, and he often thrilled us with his spectacular stunts that he would perform with his aeroplane. The reason that he came here so often was that he was engaged to a French girl here in* [censored], *and every couple of weeks he would fly over to see her....I believe I wrote you once before about an aviator who had done some particularly fine flying here—that was Quentin Roosevelt, and since we are the closest company to the flying field, it was our privilege to feel that we had more than an ordinary interest in him.*[51]

Sergeant Snyder was about to get a promotion to a commissioned officer when the armistice was signed, ending the First World War. In his last letter from France before he returned home, he wrote to his father to "give my love to all the home folks and tell them that before they know it we may be sailing home, and to have the fatted calf fat and ready, for we will be lean and also ready."[52]

If one travels to Shepherdstown today, there is a small plaque on the front of a brick building located on German Street. This is the war memorial building, and the plaque lists various Shepherdstown residents who perished during various wars. For World War I, two names are listed: Wilmer B. Miller and Thomas C. Reinhart. Wilmer Miller was a co-owner of the Owens & Miller drugstore in town. When the war started, Miller wanted to do his part and enlisted in the Army Medical School in Washington, D.C. While doing his duty for his country, he married Olive LaDelto Patriquin. On October 6, 1918, Wilmer B. Miller died of Spanish influenza. Thomas Reinhart was a prominent and well-liked young man of Shepherdstown, and it was with much enthusiasm that he joined the service in the First World War. While stationed at Camp Meade, Maryland, Thomas became the ordnance sergeant. When Spanish influenza hit the camp, Thomas became gravely ill and fought the disease for nearly two weeks before succumbing on October 14, 1918. While many in Shepherdstown made sacrifices for the world war, these men sacrificed the most.[53]

Chapter 2

SHEPHERD COLLEGE

In 1871, Shepherdstown was still struggling to recover from the Civil War that had ended six years before. After the war had ended, the large courthouse building in the middle of town was the new location for the county seat since the courthouse in Charles Town was too heavily damaged. But by 1871, the county seat had returned to Charles Town, and the large building in the middle of town had become vacant. With the future of the town at stake, leaders looked to put the vacant building to work as a school. The future of the town would be a center for education. By 1872, the state of West Virginia had approved Shepherd College as a normal school, with 42 students under the leadership of Joseph McMurran.[54] More than forty years later, the school had grown dramatically with an enrollment of 1,082 students, completely revitalizing the town.[55]

By 1914, the college had grown not only in the number of students attending it but also in the number of buildings found on campus. That original building that was the old courthouse was still in use and was known as the Old College Building. Today, that building is called McMurran Hall and is still a focal point for both the university and town. Attached to the Old College Building was a large auditorium called Shepherd College Hall. The building is today called Reynolds Hall. Not far from these buildings, on the opposite side of High Street, was the social sciences building. This building was much larger and featured classrooms, labs and a preschool where college students learned to teach. This building no longer exists today. The men's dormitory had been located on German Street in what

Left: McMurran Hall, the original building of Shepherd College. 1912. *Shepherd University Archives.*

Below: The Shepherd College Social Science building (no longer standing). 1912. *Shepherd University Archives.*

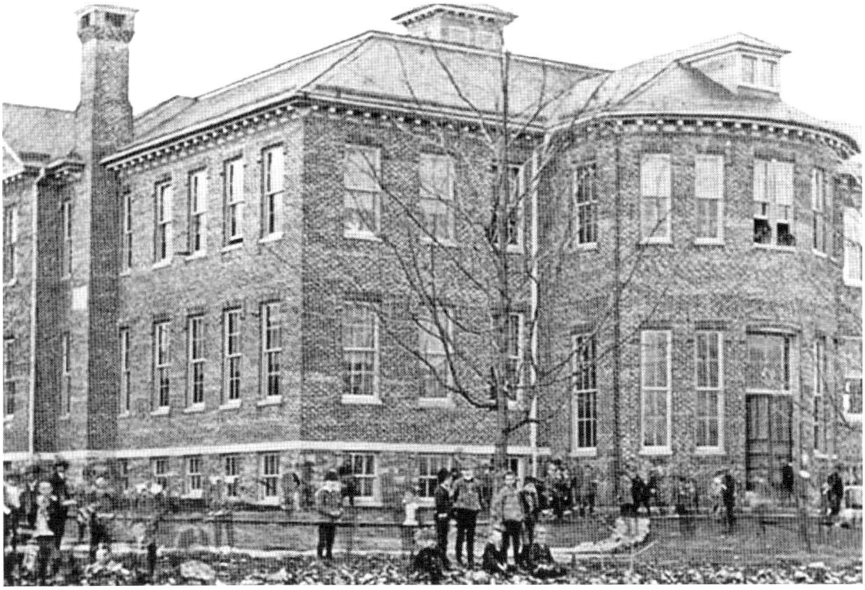

was known as Thomas Shepherd Hall (today the Entler Hotel), but a fire in 1912 likely shuttered this building—it is unclear where the dormitory would have been moved to.[56]

The main building on campus, however, was the Administration Building. Today, this is Knutti Hall. In 1914, this building had a variety uses, rooms and tools to help students succeed. The basement of the building featured a small gymnasium for students to use. On another floor was located the college library. Labs, offices and lecture halls were also found scattered throughout the building, making the Administration Building the most diverse as far as its uses on the growing campus.[57]

Top: Knutti Hall on Shepherd College's campus. 1914. *Shepherd University Archives.*

Middle: Shepherd College's gymnasium, located in the basement of Knutti Hall. 1907. *Shepherd University Archives.*

Below: The Shepherd College agricultural lab, located in Knutti Hall. 1918. *Shepherd University Archives.*

Students had a wide variety of classes and studies to choose from during their time at Shepherd College. One of the largest fields of study found at the college was teaching. When Shepherd College was originally founded, it was a teachers' college, and those roots had really grown to make Shepherd College one of the premier schools to attend for education in the early twentieth century. There was also a heavy focus on agricultural studies at the college. It makes sense that many students would find this as an area of interest since the college was located in the center of a rural region, and many students would likely go on to work in agricultural fields following their completion of studies at the college. English and writing was another field that was heavily studied at the college and one in which students were very active. The college had three literary societies: the Parthenian Literary Society, the Ciceronion Literary Society and the English Club. Participation in these saw some of the highest involvement on campus, and students were often involved in all three literary societies. The literary excellence didn't end there, as many of these students also participated in writing for the school newspaper, the *Shepherd Picket*, and the school yearbook, the *Chatonderoga*.

While students worked hard in their classes during the fall of 1914, the Great War was raging in Europe. This seemed to gain little or no attention from the campus community. Perhaps students were too focused on their studies to be bothered with the terrible events taking place so far away. The school newspaper didn't even acknowledge the war until an editorial article that was written in December of that year:

> *The Christmas season is at hand. Examinations are over and all are at home, free from the trials of our life at school, for a time at least. Now is the time when gifts are exchanged as evidences of brotherly friendship and love, when all the world is merry and gay. There is almost no Christmas this year for the people of the nations involved in war.*[58]

Most articles, however, talked about the prosperity that the state of West Virginia was seeing in the early twentieth century. It seemed to most students that Europe was tearing itself apart, and if America were to stay out of the conflict of the Great War, the country would continue to prosper.

Shepherd College's manual training shop, located in Knutti Hall. 1916. *Shepherd University Archives.*

Left: Bird's-eye view of Shepherd College. 1901. *Shepherd University Archives.*

Below: Designs for Miller Hall. 1915. *Shepherd University Archives.*

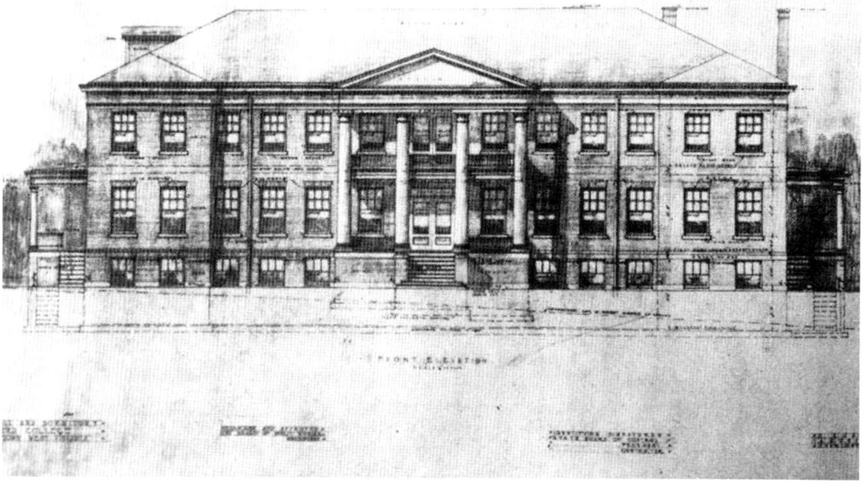

In 1916, there was great excitement to be found on the Shepherd College campus. It was announced that there would be a new building added to the campus. Located on the west side of Duke Street would be, for the first time on Shepherd's campus, a women's dormitory. The building featured large pillars leading to the front entrance, and the large brick building could house forty-four women. In honor of the Shepherd College president at the time, Thomas C. Miller, the building would be called Miller Hall. Today, this building still exists with the same name. There are still dormitories found in the building, as well as the residence life offices.[59]

In 1916, attitudes toward the European war and America's military preparedness seemed to change as well. The change in tone likely came from an increase of disdain for the Central Powers and Germany, in particular ever since the sinking of the *Lusitania*. Also, in 1916, American forces under John Pershing crossed the Mexican border to search for the rebel Pancho Villa, who had raided several American towns. The action showed that America had little military preparedness in the event that the country should

Completed Miller Hall. 1917. *Shepherd University Archives.*

The Shepherd College art studio, located in Knutti Hall. 1918. *Shepherd University Archives.*

be thrust into war. One student who likely noticed this wrote an article called "Preparedness" in which he claimed that "we predict war and if you belong to the pacifist body you are in dire danger of being overwhelmed by the advancing foe."[60] The college's Young Men's Christian Association (YMCA) also released a poem around this time called "The Two Calls":

Young men wanted for the army,
To carry on the cannonade;
Young men wanted for the army,
To come to the nation's aid.[61]

Looking back to what these students published, it is now clear that they saw the path that the United States was on, heading toward entering the world war.

It is possible that many students had this in mind in 1916 when the elections took place. Woodrow Wilson ran on the platform of keeping the country out of the war, and for college students, who were in the age range of young adults who typically were the ones to join the military during times of war, that likely weighed heavily on their minds. The election season also brought exciting news to the campus: John J. Cornwell had been elected governor of the state of West Virginia. Cornwell was a graduate of Shepherd College, and all felt overwhelming pride to have a prestigious alumnus heading the state. The celebration was short-lived, however, because soon after the inauguration of the president and governor, the nation found itself being plunged into war.

Governor John J. Cornwell, a Shepherd College alumni. 1917. *Shepherd University Archives.*

When America entered the First World War, the most immediate impact felt on the Shepherd College campus came when Governor Cornwell put out a request for farmers to prioritize food production. Since Shepherd's agricultural programs were such a high priority, bringing in farmers from all over the region, the college did something unprecedented. The college allowed these students to leave. The patriotic duties of the country came before the college's need to increase student population and income from tuition payments. An initial group of nineteen farmers left the school to put their full efforts into food production for the war. These farmers were honored in the *Shepherd Picket* with a student-submitted poem titled "To Those Who Left Us":

When came the call their country to support,
These noble youths did deem it to but their share,
To aid the nation with their small part,
Though not in battles of the land or air.

Top: Farmers, honored here, left school to tend to the fields. 1917. *Shepherd University Archives.*

Bottom: The Shepherd College chemistry lab, located Knutti Hall. 1918. *Shepherd University Archives.*

Truly their part they thought could best be done,
On many a farm where first they found a bed,
Tilling the land that battles may be won,
By others, who their toil has amply fed.[62]

Another contribution that Shepherd College made toward the war effort was the massive participation in both the YMCA and the YWCA (Young Women's Christian Association). Immediately, these organizations pledged to help their national organizations raise $35 million toward the war effort. Together, these organizations on the Shepherd College campus decided that a reasonable goal for the college to help the national goal would be raising $500. On October 24, 1917, the two groups decided to go forth with a fundraising campaign to meet their goal, and before they even started, President Thomas C. Miller announced that members of the faculty would donate $25. By noon that day, the associations had raised $730.50 toward the war effort, far exceeding their goal. The school newspaper praised the campaign: "It certainly is an expression of the patriotism and self-sacrifice of the students that has never been equaled before in the history of the school, and we justly commend the entire organization of good old S.C. for its splendid work in the campaign."[63]

The patriotic movement on campus was not restricted just to the farmers and YMCA/YWCA members. Feelings of patriotism spread throughout the student body and faculty. Many students submitted essays and poems to the school newspaper in order to do their part in keeping the student body thinking about what they can do for the war effort. One student submitted an essay titled "We Fight for Alsace-Lorraine." In this essay, the student explores the history of these provinces, which had several times switched between French and German state control. The most recent switch had occurred in 1871, when after the Franco-Prussian War the Germans demanded the territories be placed under their control. The essay then pointed out that after a year of involvement in the war, President Woodrow Wilson had made comments regarding the territories in which he noted that "all French territory should be freed and restored, and the wrong done to France by Prussia in 1871 in the matter of Alsace-Lorraine, which has unsettled the peace of the world for nearly fifty years, should be righted, in order that peace may once more be made secure in the interests of all." The author then finished by informing the Shepherd College students:

> *The world has not been safe for liberty loving people since 1870, and President Wilson is right when he says that Alsace and Lorraine must be restored to France, a part of which government they long to be. All arguments about past ownership or past strife are beside the point. If we had been more thoughtful, we would have recognized at once a promise that our hope for their restoration would be fulfilled, when America entered the Great War to "make the world safe for democracy."*[64]

Of course, Shepherd College had a more immediate impact on the war than just fundraising and patriotism. Many Shepherd students and alumni decided to serve their country by joining the military. In total, by the end of the war, 203 Shepherd College students and alumni had joined the service.[65]

The Shepherd College domestic sciences lab, located in Knutti Hall. 1918. *Shepherd University Archives.*

Shepherd College veterans pose for a photo in uniform. 1919. *Shepherd University Archives.*

The school kept close tabs on those members of the Shepherd College community who joined the military, and their stories were published in every issue of the *Shepherd Picket*. The faculty and campus leaders were very proud of the service provided by their community and released this statement to all the men who served in the armed forces at the close of the war:

> *A large percentage of these boys went overseas, but those who were in the various camps in this country were as patriotic and as willing to serve as those who were more fortunate, as they look upon it, in going abroad. We want to congratulate you, one and all, for the patriotic spirit and*

> *loyal service rendered to the Government in this, the greatest of all world conflicts. Whether private or commissioned officer, whether in a cantonment in America or in the battlefield of France, you are entitled to the gratitude of a republic which lent its aid in crushing autocracy and upholding the principles of democracy for which our forefathers contended.*[66]

The first Shepherd College community member to make it overseas was not a male combatant—it was Anna Gardiner. Gardiner had graduated from Shepherd College in 1909 and after graduation had moved to New Bedford, Massachusetts, where she was an instructor of nurses at St. Luke's Hospital. Upon the entry of the United States in the First World War, Anna joined the service as a nurse and went overseas, where she served at U.S. Base Hospital 6.[67] Anna was always very proud of her service in France and worked fiercely to help the soldiers under her charge. In one of her letters home, she said, "We are still making dressings, and as each one does only a part and the same part it becomes very monotonous. We make a game of it though, in trying to see how many we can make in one day." She selflessly asked for friends and family to send supplies—not for her, but for the soldiers. "Send some tooth-brushes for the boys—the cheapest here cost about fifty to seventy cents."[68] It is unclear just how many men Anna would have had to help treat, but one can only imagine the horrible wounds she would have seen. It is doubtless that the bravery of her actions certainly saved many lives.

William Clayton Myers. 1917. *Shepherd University Archives.*

The first student to leave school in order to serve in the military was William Clayton Myers, who was in the midst of his senior year at Shepherd College when he enlisted in 1917. Myers enlisted in the Hospital Corps of the Navy in May 1917 at Hagerstown, Maryland. As Myers went through training, he sent home letters talking about his experiences and successes. He was very excited to report at one point that he had "shaved a man without drawing blood and put in a few stitches without causing pain, but do not be alarmed, the man was dead."[69] When Myers received word that he would be transferred to League Island for overseas duty, he simply reported, "I do not know how long I will be in this country."[70] Soon after this, Myers became stationed on the USS *Henderson*, which would make more than a dozen round trips to and from Europe. Needless to say, William got his sea legs under him. His first action on the boat came when a fire broke out on the ship, and he was rushed to the area to see if anyone was overcome by the fire and smoke. Myers did witness a submarine fight and described the action and the end of the war as follows:

Guy Crigler. 1912. *Shepherd University Archives.*

> *We had a submarine fight off the coast of Delaware on the night of August the 13th, 1918, and went aground on the night of August the twenty-eighth. On September 28th, 1918, at about 12:05 A.M. the U.S.S. Finland collided with the Henderson, which she struck three times: first amid the ship, second off the port beam, third over port propellers. We were in Brest, at the time of the signing of the armistice. The American, French and English vessels took part in the celebration. The aircraft that was there also took part in it. The harbor fortifications celebrated until midnight....It was certainly a wonderful sight.*[71]

Guy Crigler graduated from Shepherd College in 1912. Wanting to do his part, Guy decided to enlist in the Marine Corps on January 27, 1918. He trained at Paris Island, South Carolina, and Quantico, Virginia. His unit left for Europe on April 23, 1918. Upon his arrival in France, Crigler was placed in the Eighty-Second Company, Sixth Regiment, United States Marine Corps. This set up Guy to be right in the thick of a battle that would go down in Marine Corps history as one that would forever change how the branch operated. Up until the First World War, the United States Marine Corps had always acted under the U.S. Navy, usually (with a few exceptions) acting as a force on ships to guard the captains from mutiny and boarding enemy ships. When General Pershing, in charge of the AEF, needed more ground troops in France, he brought in U.S. marines to serve in the Second Division of the AEF. On June 6, 1918, Guy Crigler stepped off with his fellow marines into an attack at the German-held Belleau Wood. The battle was hard fought, but the marines proved that they could hold their own when it came to fighting on land. From that time forward, the Marine Corps would comprise land combatants and act almost as its own branch of service (though still technically under the United States Navy). Guy Crigler fought in this battle until July 12, 1918, when he was severely wounded. After this, he was transferred from hospital to hospital until he eventually made it back to the United States in September 1918 and was honorably discharged from service on February 23, 1919.[72]

C. Wardell McDonald was a Shepherd College student who had a similar experience to Guy Crigler. McDonald trained for the military at Charles Town, West Virginia. On August 21, 1918, C. Wardell sailed for France, where he joined Company E of the 360th Infantry Regiment, 77th Division. With the 306th, McDonald participated in the Meuse-Argonne Offensive, the largest American offensive of the entire war—it is still the bloodiest battle in American history. On November 1, in the midst of an especially large battle, C. Wardell McDonald was wounded, taken off the line and sent from hospital to hospital in order to recover. He arrived back in the United States on March 24, 1919, and was honorably discharged from Camp Sherman on May 23, 1919.[73]

One of the Shepherd College boys who arguably saw the most action throughout the First World War was Henry B. Reinhart. Reinhart enlisted in the military on April 14, 1917, just eight days after the United States entered the Great War. Reinhart trained with the Nineteenth Infantry Regiment until he reached the rank of lieutenant. Having soared from enlisted man to commissioned officer so quickly, Lieutenant Reinhart was then transferred to the Fourth Infantry Regiment, which was more prepared for frontline service. Henry sailed for France on April 6, 1918, and during service in the AEF, he saw action in almost every major campaign by American service personnel. He fought in the Aisne Defensive, Marne Defensive, Marne Offensive (all of these can be considered part of the Aisne-Marne Offensive), the St. Mihiel Offensive and the Meuse-Argonne Offensive. After the armistice was signed on November 11, 1918, Lieutenant Reinhart moved from unit to unit, serving in the Army of Occupation until he was sent back to the United States in May 1919, officially being discharged on June 10, 1919.[74]

Shepherd College students and alumni experienced great successes in the Great War. But not all those who served would make it home. Shepherd would have thirteen gold stars added to its service flag representing those Shepherd College students and alumni who perished in the First World War. This number included Wilmer B. Miller and Thomas C. Reinhart, who were also honored by members of the Shepherdstown community. To

Aisne-Marne American Cemetery. *Author's collection.*

mourn the sacrifice that Shepherd College had made during the Great War, the *Shepherd Picket* printed the poem "Stars of Gold" by Waitman Barbe, which was written to honor the West Virginia university men who perished in the war:

With cheers for every star, we flung
Our flag a year ago and sung
The songs of marching men:
And all the season through
We proudly filled the flag with stars
Until they crowded field and bars,
And still we cheer'd for then
Our stars were all of blue.

But now in silence do we raise
Another flag too dear for praise,
And every head we bow
And for awhile withhold
Our cheers for banners filled with blue:
Another color shineth through
The field and bars—for now
These stars have turned to gold.[75]

Ira Moser Derr graduated from Shepherd College in 1910. Upon receiving his degree, he went on to enroll in the Richmond Medical School. After getting his degree from Richmond, he took over the Sheltering Arms Hospital in Hansford, West Virginia. On June 3, 1918, he married Gene Simms. A little over a month later, Ira Derr entered service with the Medical Corps at Camp Wadsworth, where he received a commission as

Dr. Ira Derr. 1910. *Shepherd University Archives.*

first lieutenant. On November 6, 1918, just a few days before the armistice was signed and a few hours before he would be promoted to the rank of captain, Dr. Ira Derr succumbed to pneumonia.[76]

Thomas F. Ewers attended Shepherd College from 1911 to 1912. Henry Luckett Clapham graduated from Shepherd College in 1915. While it is unclear whether these two men knew each other during their experiences at Shepherd, both men ended up entering service at the Army Training School in Richmond, Virginia, on July 13, 1918. Later, both men were transferred to Camp Colt in Gettysburg, Pennsylvania, the same training camp where Dwight D. Eisenhower was stationed. Both men ended up contracting Spanish influenza and died within hours of each other on October 4, 1918.[77]

J. Rodney Power volunteered to go to the United States Army Training School in Richmond, Virginia, on June 26, 1918. From there, Power transferred to Romney, West Virginia, to continue his training on July 13, 1918. On September 13, 1918, Rodney once again transferred, this time to the Texas Agricultural and Mechanical College in Texas. There he contracted Spanish influenza. He died from the disease on October 13, 1918. His remains were brought to his home in Levels, West Virginia, to be buried.[78]

Marshall Earle Martin graduated from Shepherd College in 1915 and was a captain in the West Virginia infantry. He was the first Shepherd College alumni to die, succumbing to pneumonia on May 12, 1917, one month into the war. John C. Gochenour was training in Battery E of the 313th Field Artillery at Camp Lee when he contracted pneumonia and perished on February 7, 1918. William Bryan Swisher entered service at Camp Lee, Virginia, on September 3, 1918. Within twelve days, Swisher had come down with Spanish influenza, which then brought bronchial pneumonia with it. This complication caused his death on September 26, 1918.[79]

Washington Berry Grove was perhaps one of the oldest Shepherd College alumni to serve in the First World War, having graduated in 1889. His post-college career was a long, continuous service in the United

Left: Henry Lucket Clapham. 1915. *Shepherd University Archives.*

Right: Marshall Earle Martin. 1915. *Shepherd University Archives.*

States Navy as a member of the Medical Corps. Grove was considered to be one of the hardest-working medical staff members ever since the United States entered the war. He survived the war only to die a few months later of disease on January 21, 1919. Kenna McCarta Weber was a student at Shepherd College in 1912. When the war began, Weber joined Company I, Seventh Infantry Regiment, Third Division, AEF. With this unit, Weber saw considerable action in France, specifically at the Battle of Chateau-Theirry and the Aisne-Marne Offensive. While Weber was able to avoid being wounded or killed by the enemy, he succumbed to illness on September 8, 1918.[80]

Another Shepherd College student who saw action in France was Hubert Monroe Phares. Phares was a champion long-distance runner at Shepherd College and was remembered vividly for it. He entered the Auto Mechanical School on May 1, 1918, and was trained at Richmond, Virginia. Soon he was selected for active duty in France with the Twenty-First Supply Company, Field Artillery. With this unit, he was wounded in the summer of 1918. Complications from these wounds led to pneumonia, which ultimately killed him on September 2, 1918.[81]

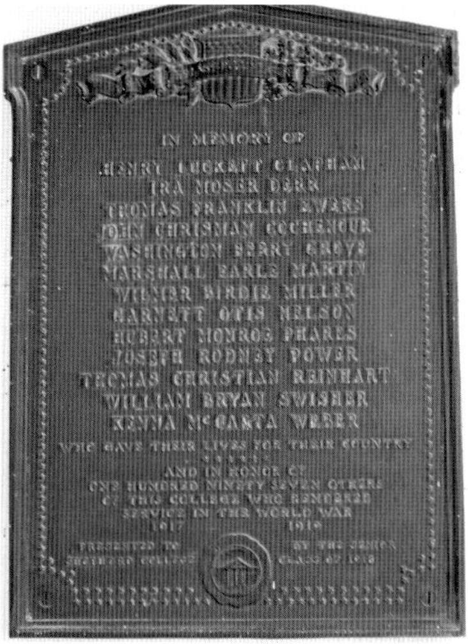

Above: American monument at Château-Thierry, France. *Author's collection.*

Right, top: Garnet Otis Nelson's class picture from 1914. *Shepherd University Archives.*

Right, bottom: Plaque on the entrance to Knutti Hall to Shepherd students killed in World War I. *Author's collection.*

Garnett Otis Nelson graduated from Shepherd College in 1914 and afterward spent his career as a teacher and principal, looking to have a positive influence on the children of West Virginia. Nelson enlisted in the armed services on May 25, 1918, and trained at Camp Lee, where he reached the rank of corporal. He sailed for France on July 18, 1918, and soon after was promoted to sergeant. In August, Sergeant Nelson was on his way to the front lines when he was hit by a truck, severely wounding his right hand and leg. After two months in the hospital, he returned to his comrades in Company M of the Sixteenth Infantry Regiment, First Division. On October 16, 1918, in the midst of the Meuse-Argonne Offensive, Garnett Nelson was wounded and gassed. He was rushed to a hospital in Paris but succumbed to these wounds on November 15, 1918, four days after the armistice was signed.[82]

Soon after the war ended, the *Shepherd Picket* began advocating for some sort of memorial to the memory of those who served in the Great War.

An article proffered the possibility of a memorial hall or library that could further benefit society in the name of the brave men. But if that were not possible, then the author of the article had another idea as to how to honor the men—with a tablet:

> *As our old college building was given to the town as a center of social uplift, there could be no more appropriate place for such tablets than in that beautiful, historical old structure. It is now home to the Daughters of the American Revolution, and could very appropriately be made the meeting place of the returned soldiers of this section of the county.*[83]

While the *Shepherd Picket* would not get its wish for a location for a memorial tablet, the class of 1918 donated a tablet to the Shepherd College students and alumni who served in the First World War, to be placed in their honor at the front entrance of the Administration Building.

Chapter 3

HARPERS FERRY

In the 1700s, a man by the name of Robert Harper was traveling west when he came through an area that was nicknamed "The Hole." The area of land described was a peninsula formed by the convergence of the Potomac and Shenandoah Rivers. On the opposite side of the rivers from the peninsula were the Blue Ridge Mountains. The peninsula rapidly rose in elevation and extended to the south and west, becoming what is now known as the Shenandoah Valley. Harper looked at the landscape around him and instantly fell in love. He purchased a ferry in the location from a squatter by the name of Peter Stephens and, eventually, large portions of the surrounding land from Lord Fairfax. Thus, Harpers Ferry was founded.

Slowly, people began to move into the area, but after the American Revolution, the nation's first president made a decision that would forever change the history of Harpers Ferry, as well as what would become of Jefferson County, West Virginia. George Washington wanted to place one of the government's armories (a factory that makes guns) and arsenals (where guns are stored) right in the location of this small town. Washington's reasoning was simple: the mountains were covered in trees that could be used as gun stocks as well as charcoal, iron deposits nearby could be used for gun barrels, the location was close enough to what would become the nation's capital that the weapons could be moved to the defense of the city (but far enough upstream that foreign navies could not reach it) and the waters of the two rivers could be harnessed to power machinery. The

Jefferson Rock at Harpers Ferry. 1912. *Harpers Ferry National Historical Park.*

population of the small ferry town blossomed as people rushed to the jobs the factory provided.

The factory required hundreds of workers to make the guns by hand until a gentleman by the name of John Hall signed a contract with the government in 1819 to begin developing his machine-made rifles in a factory along the Shenandoah River at Harpers Ferry. Soon his technology made it down the street to the other government gun factory. The technology allowed, for the first time in history, the ability to have interchangeable parts. The American system of manufacturing was born, and Harpers Ferry was the epicenter of the American Industrial Revolution and the technology that came to define the nineteenth century. The population continued to boom as both the C&O Canal and B&O Railroad made their way through the town. It seemed that if anyone in the mid-Atlantic region of the United States wanted to travel west, they would almost have to travel through Harpers Ferry.

However, the success was not destined to last in Harpers Ferry. In 1859, an abolitionist by the name of John Brown and his small band of followers attacked the government's arsenal and armory in an attempt to gather weapons to free the slaves of the South. Brown's attempt failed and he was later hanged in Charles Town for his actions, but his actions sent a clear message that the country was so divided on the issue of slavery that it was being led down a path toward conflict. Harpers Ferry was no longer the famous industrial town that acted as a gateway to the west, but rather the infamous town where Brown either was captured trying to do what was right or was thwarted in his plan of mass murder.

When Virginia seceded in 1861, the governor sent three hundred Virginia militia to the town to capture the arsenal and armory. The roughly forty-five United States soldiers stationed there to guard the government complex decided to destroy what they could not defend. The arsenal building was blown up, and the factories were set ablaze. While most of the machinery was saved, Confederate general Thomas Jackson decided to send it south for use by the Confederacy. This was just the start of the destruction that Harpers Ferry would see in the war to come. With the main source of jobs gone, most of the citizens left the town, reducing a population of roughly three thousand to between one hundred and three hundred. The town remained a vital location for various campaigns and would end up changing hands eight times, many times through battle. By the end of the war, Harpers Ferry was left in ruin.

Reconstruction began to take over in Harpers Ferry, but the town didn't seem to be growing. Factories attempted to reoccupy Virginius Island, but the town was not returning to the industrial epicenter it once was. This was due, in part, to the geography. Harpers Ferry is located at the lowest point in all of West Virginia, between the Shenandoah and Potomac Rivers; it is entirely on a floodplain. When factories attempted to settle in the town, very often they would get swept away. A flood in 1870 was one of the town's largest and killed fifty people. After Reconstruction, it looked like there might be some hope for Harpers Ferry.

The government began selling its holdings in Harpers Ferry, and various businesses began to move in to try and revitalize the old armory grounds. The B&O Railroad even bought an area known as Byrne's Island, where it put a small amusement park known as Island Park that began to attract many visitors. The park seemed to at least generate excitement and hope in Harpers Ferry once more. In the 1880s and '90s, the B&O Railroad improved its tracks in the Harpers Ferry area, including building a railroad tunnel through the mountain known as Maryland Heights and a new train station on the old armory grounds, allowing for easier travel to the town. By the turn of the century, the town looked vastly different from the ruins that were left over from the end of the Civil War.[84]

Slowly but surely, the town's economy looked toward tourism. Where after the Civil War agriculture was the driving factor of the Harpers

View of Harpers Ferry, West Virginia, from Camp Hill. 1910. *Harpers Ferry National Historical Park.*

Ferry economy, by 1900, only 5 percent of the population of the town was listed as being farmers, whereas it had been as high as 20 percent at one point.[85] In 1914, the famous Hill Top House, a hotel located at the top of Camp Hill that overlooked the confluence of the Potomac and Shenandoah Rivers, was advertising single-room rates of twelve dollars per week and double rooms at twenty dollars per week. The advertisement said of the hotel:

> *The above Hotel, with improved service in every department is open to the public. Rooms with and without private baths. Meals are noted and the location of this beautiful Hotel makes it one of the most attractive in this community. Charges are reasonable. Special attention given in winter months to dance parties, and we are prepared to furnish everything.*[86]

At the same time, the Island Park was looking for the opportunity to increase revenue from the tourists. The amusement park included live entertainment, brass bands, picnic areas and food vendors. Gilbert Perry, a lifelong resident of the town, called the amusement park "every bit as gay as Coney Island."[87]

In dealing with the increased visitation, the town improved roads and buildings to attract more tourists to the beauty of the town. These improvements, which took place in the 1880s and 1890s, included the renovations on the famous St. Peter's Catholic Church. The structure had been put in place in the 1830s and was on high ground so it could be seen from almost anywhere in town. The renovations made the church look almost Gothic, as if the structure had been transported straight from Europe. By the twentieth century, the town no longer looked like a town still reeling from the destruction of war but rather a quaint hamlet in the midst of some of the most beautiful natural and man-made scenery.[88]

One such attraction to the town, for both locals and tourists, was the famous Jefferson Rock. It is on this rock that Thomas Jefferson supposedly got the inspiration to write this passage in his book *Notes on the State of Virginia* in 1785:

> *The passage of the Patowmac through the Blue Ridge is perhaps one of the most stupendous scenes in Nature. You stand on a very high point of land. On your right comes up the Shenandoah, having ranged along the foot of the mountain a hundred miles to seek a vent. On your left approaches the Patowmac in quest of a passage also. In the moment of their junction they rush together against the mountain, rend it asunder and pass off to the sea. The first glance of this scene hurries our senses into the opinion that this earth has been created in time, that the mountains were formed first, that the rivers began to flow afterwards, that in this place particularly they have been so dammed up by the Blue Ridge of mountains as to have formed an ocean which filled the whole valley; that, continuing to rise, they have at last broken over at this spot and have torn the mountain down from its summit to its base. The piles of rock on each hand, but particularly on the Shenandoah, the evident marks of their disruptions and avulsions from their beds by the most powerful agents in nature, corroborate the impression.…It is worth a voyage across the Atlantic.*[89]

During the Industrial Revolution at Harpers Ferry, this view was largely ruined by smokestacks and coal smoke filling the air. However, by 1914, none of the factories that had come to the town could even come close to the size and scope of the government facilities that had existed before the war. Jefferson Rock's view was restored and was now partially framed by the new steeple from the renovations of St. Peter's. The natural beauty of the

Above: National Guard units on parade through Harpers Ferry, West Virginia, on Shenandoah Street. 1908. *Harpers Ferry National Historical Park.*

Right: A family visiting Jefferson Rock. 1917. *Jefferson County Historical Society.*

area had been restored, and the rock remained a major attraction through the First World War and is still a natural beauty today.

One sight that Harpers Ferry had become accustomed to throughout its history was that of soldiers occupying the area. Camp Hill in town had gotten its name from United States soldiers camping there in the early days of the armory's existence. All throughout the Civil War, the town was occupied by troops of whichever army happened to control it at the time. Some of these forces, such as the brigade under Stonewall Jackson, used the heights above the twin town of Bolivar to train their troops. In the early twentieth century, this tradition of soldiers stationed at Harpers Ferry would continue. The Washington, D.C., National Guard looked for several areas to train its troops outside the nation's capital.

As early as 1908, the D.C. National Guard began training on the same grounds as the famous Stonewall Brigade, calling the area "Camp Ordway." The land today is known as "Bolivar Heights" and the "Murphey-Chambers Farm." At the time, the farm was simply known as the Murphey Farm, and it should be noted that the farm is on the same ridge line as Bolivar Heights. The D.C. National Guard spent its summers in this location for several reasons, but it is likely that one of the main reasons was that the battles fought at Harpers Ferry during the Civil War were largely influenced by terrain, so the area could impart valuable geographic lessons to the National Guard members. Soldiers at the camp learned several drills ranging from artillery to small arms, wireless radio and marching. The citizens of Harpers Ferry loved the presence of the National Guard troops in their town. The men offered more customers for the shops and restaurants in town and provided just one more attraction to the tourists. The National Guard Band would give performances that citizens would come out and watch; a woman by the name of Isabel Flanagan seemed to enjoy the presence of troops, saying, "It was interesting to watch them drill from our porch high above the hill."[90] The D.C. National Guard stopped coming to Camp Ordway in roughly 1913–14, before America had entered the First World War, but the camp would be a constant reminder to the people of Jefferson County what life was like for their sons and brothers going off to war just three years later.

Another development that the town saw at this time was the growth of public education for children. Before 1912, students in Harpers Ferry had a few options as to how to get an education. One of the least liked options was for students to travel by train to schools in either Brunswick, Maryland, or Martinsburg, West Virginia. The train tickets were expensive and the commutes too far. Others opted for a private school education, for which they had two choices: a private school run by Miss Alvernon Cross and one run by Miss Annie Marmion. Annie Marmion would later become locally famous in the 1950s when her childhood diary detailing life in Civil War Harpers Ferry was published as *Under Fire*. Annie Marmion's school was run out of her childhood home on Public Way. Today, some employees at Harpers Ferry refer to these buildings as "Marmion Row," attached to the Harper House, the oldest building in Harpers Ferry. In 1912, the lack of options for citizens of Harpers Ferry to send their children to school was solved when Harpers Ferry High School was built. The first graduating class of the high school was in 1915 and had two students: Gladys Marlatt and Louise Newcomer. The next class, in 1916, had four graduates: Agnes Buzzard, Cora Rockenbaugh, Eliza Shugart and Earl Stabs. By 1917, the graduating class had seven students.[91]

With a new high school, an expanding tourism draw and improved infrastructure, Harpers Ferry was very clearly on the rise. The town looked to be on the path toward returning to the large successful town of more than fifty years earlier. It is likely because of this that many in the town looked at the announcement in April 1917 that the United States would enter the world war with dread. War would mean that fewer people would travel, hurting Harpers Ferry's new tourist economy. In addition, any work on continuing to improve the infrastructure of the town and expand it would have to be put on hold. All materials for such work would have to be prioritized for the war effort. Those who had lived in the town during the Civil War had enough of war and violence and wanted nothing to do with the war effort.

Regardless of the implications that war meant for Harpers Ferry, the citizens still wanted to keep a close eye on their sons who would go off to war, as well as the efforts made by the rest of the county. Harpers Ferry even found great interest in how relatives of their most famous visitor had decided to pick up arms for the country's war effort. An article in January 1918 noted:

> *Three great-grandsons of John Brown, the Harper's Ferry raider, are in the U.S. Navy. R.B. Chamberlain, one of them, is at the Mare Island Navy yard, while the other two, John Brown, of Seattle, and John Scott, of Portland, are on battleships. The two last-named are grandsons of Salmon Brown, the only living son of John Brown.*[92]

It would be Harpers Ferry that would feel the sting of war first in Jefferson County. Daniel B. Newcomer was the son of one of the Storer College professors. Newcomer was eighteen years old, and in the fall after the United States entered the war, he applied for admission into aviation school for the army. He went to Washington, D.C., to take an examination, and after he passed it, he was sent to camp at San Antonio, Texas, for training. Several weeks after he arrived, he contracted measles, which then developed into pneumonia. When Daniel's condition became worse, his parents were notified and immediately made plans to visit their son. Mr. Newcomer was in the midst of traveling south to San Antonio when he received a telegram that his son had passed. Two weeks later, Daniel's body was brought home to Harpers Ferry, and following a service at the

The Harpers Ferry High School class of 1917. Daniel Newcommer is located in the third row from the bottom, far left. *Harpers Ferry National Historical Park.*

Methodist church in Bolivar, Daniel B. Newcomer was laid to rest at Harper Cemetery, where he still is today.[93]

While Daniel Newcomer made the ultimate sacrifice, Daniel H. Nichols made another type of sacrifice. Mr. Nichols, a citizen of Harpers Ferry, watched all three of his sons join the military in the First World War. The last of these boys was his youngest son, Joseph Nichols. One of his sons was Daniel S. Nichols, who served overseas as part of the Base Hospital Units. He spent most of the war in LeHavre, France, taking care of the sick and wounded. He survived the war and was discharged from service on May 1, 1919.[94]

One Bolivar man had a curious story after he was drafted in the war. James Henry Bagent was drafted in the spring of 1918, and soon afterward, this article was printed about him in the *Shepherdstown Register*:

> *Last week James Henry Bagent, of Bolivar, this county, was among the drafted men sent from Jefferson County to Columbus Barracks, Ohio. He took a good look at the place after arriving there, and then jumped the first freight train for home. The local draft board heard of his safe arrival here and ordered his arrest. Town Sergeant Robert Shipley, of Shepherdstown, went after him and found him at home, though Mr. Bagent acted in a real unobtrusive way, and brought him to this place and lodged him in jail last Friday night. Monday he took the prisoner to Camp Meade and turned him over to the proper authorities, who will try to hold him. Bagent said that he didn't mind going to Camp Meade, but he was sure opposed to Columbus.*[95]

It is unclear if James Bagent was ever released from his prison at Camp Meade before the war ended or not. And if so, it is also unclear if he was made to serve or not.

Sergeant Major William J. Geary was born in Harpers Ferry, but at the time the war broke out, he was living in Washington, D.C., working as a clerk and draftsman for the Marine Corps. William had expressed deep interest in going to France to help fight on the front lines and was granted that wish. In June, he was sent to France and immediately put on the front lines, likely at Belleau Wood. There Sergeant Major Geary was killed in battle. It is said that his mother was knitting him a sweater when she heard the news of his death.[96]

B.C. Sponseller was a native of Bolivar. He served in Company K, 317th Infantry Regiment, 80th Division. The 80th Division was nicknamed the "Blue Ridge" division, fitting for a Bolivar native. After arriving on the front

Right: Daniel Shirley Nichols. 1916. *Shepherd University Archives.*

Below: National Guard soldiers walking down High Street in Harpers Ferry. 1912. *Harpers Ferry National Historical Park.*

lines in September 1918, Sponseller was hit by a shell fragment that broke a bone in his shoulder. He wrote to his sister afterward to let her know that even though the injury was painful, he was going to fully recover.[97]

In 1919, a Storer College student wrote to the college president, Henry T. McDonald, about his experiences overseas. In the letter, the soldier mentions that while he was stationed near the Argonne Forest not long after the war

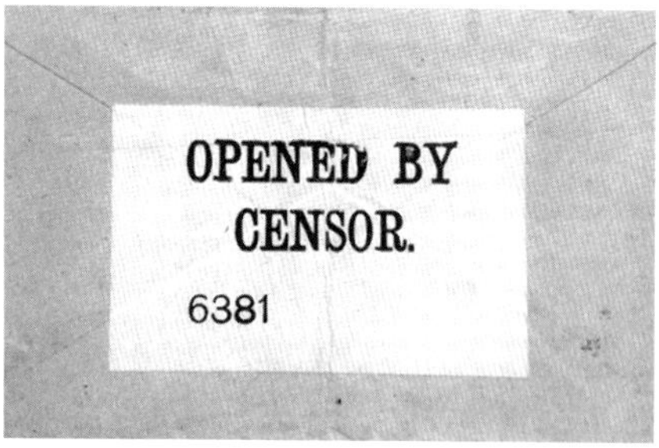

A censorship notice to show that the enveloped had been opened by the censor. *Jefferson County Historical Society.*

Photo of Jefferson County native Clarence Grove. 1918. *Jefferson County Historical Society.*

ended, he noticed something very interesting that reminded him of Harpers Ferry. "Next to my dugout was a grave with the name [censored] (Harpers Ferry). Have you heard of his death?"[98] The censorship in this letter leaves the identity of the man a mystery. To the best knowledge available, there were two soldiers who actually lived in Harpers Ferry at the time of the war and died overseas, leaving the possibility that it could be either of them. One is Clarence C. Grove, who was killed in action, and the other was John H. Fleming, who died of his wounds. Fleming has very little trace left behind of where he might have died or what unit he was with. Grove, on the other hand, was part of the 125th Infantry Regiment, 32nd Division, AEF, and was killed on October 9, 1918, in the midst of the Meuse-Argonne Offensive, making it very likely that he is the soldier buried at the grave that this Storer College student saw. Further evidence that points to Clarence Grove being in that grave is the fact that Private John Fleming is not buried overseas, meaning his body was likely sent home for burial. Private Clarence Grove, on the other hand, is currently buried in Plot D, Row 30, Grave 6 of the Meuse-Argonne American Cemetery. He was likely buried on the field close to where he fell before being transferred over to the American Cemetery. While we may never know for sure whose name was on that grave, all evidence does seem to point to Private Clarence C. Grove.[99]

While Harpers Ferry was far from the battlefields in France, death still hit home. Harpers Ferry during the Civil War had several field hospitals that

Meuse-Argonne American Cemetery. *Author's collection.*

mostly took care of soldiers who had become ill. Much of the death that occurred in Harpers Ferry in the Civil War was not from battle but rather from disease. History would end up repeating itself in the fall of 1918. As the First World War was drawing to a close, Spanish influenza hit the United States with unforgiving fury. The grisly disease spread and killed fast. Harpers Ferry residents recalled how, as the disease spread, coffins were piled up at the B&O Railroad station in town to be distributed throughout the county and even to B&O Railroad stations farther west, as the influenza was taking its toll on railroad employees. One article had this to say on the state of the B&O Railroad during this crisis: "The influenza was severe in Cumberland, and there have been hundreds of deaths in that city and the adjacent towns and countryside. Of the 5,600 men employed on the Cumberland divisions of the B&O Railroad, 3,500 were down with the influenza at one time."[100]

Death was spreading throughout the county faster than anyone could keep up with it. Many hoped that the war would never come to their doorstep, killing and destroying as it did fifty years earlier. However, while the battlefields remained an ocean away, death was brought home by the soldiers in the form of disease. One article said of the pandemic:

> *The worst epidemic of disease within the memory of the present generation is the pestilence known as the "Spanish influenza" that is now sweeping through this country....It is an exceedingly serious disease, being both contagious and infectious, and once getting a start in a community it attacks a large proportion of the population. It is something like the old grip, but is much more serious. Pneumonia frequently follows the initial symptoms and causes fatal results....* [T]*he influenza seems to have first appeared in our community last week to a noticeable extent....Monday conditions seemed to be very serious.*

Walter McGarry Duke, Shepherd College professor. 1918. *Shepherd University Archives.*

The spread of Spanish influenza was so serious that churches closed their doors and Shepherd College was forced to cancel classes, closing for weeks. Shepherd College notably lost one of its professors, Walter McGarry Duke, causing much distress and sadness in the community and on the campus.[101] The number of casualties across the globe is still uncertain, but most estimates put the number between 20 and 50 million people killed from the Spanish flu, nearly 5 percent of the world's population.

Eventually, Spanish influenza would pass, and more of the soldiers would begin to return home. Harpers Ferry was fearful at the start of the war that the road to recovery would be stopped for its town. However, despite the emergency of the Spanish flu, the town came out the other side of the war just as strong as it had been before. It continued to build on its success, expand its economy and build on its infrastructure. However, major floods in both 1924 and 1936 almost completely destroyed the town. All hope that Harpers Ferry had of becoming the thriving town it once was, was lost in the waters of the Potomac and Shenandoah Rivers. In 1944, large sections of the town were turned over to the government, becoming part of the Harpers Ferry National Monument. In 1963, the area was awarded national historical park status, becoming Harpers Ferry National Historical Park. This has preserved the town from being washed away and has almost froze it in time. Despite all the setbacks, Harpers Ferry still survives today.

Chapter 4

STORER COLLEGE AND THE AFRICAN AMERICAN COMMUNITY

Little has been said thus far of the impact that the First World War had on the African American community in Jefferson County. It should be noted that the Great War had a massive impact on this community, not only locally but nationally as well. Woodrow Wilson claimed that American involvement in the war was to make the world safe for democracy, but did this safe world have a place for minorities? Wilson has long been noted for his hypocrisy when it comes to race, specifically with his Fourteen Points claiming that national self-determination was how the world should be organized, all while he still had a strong belief in colonization. Despite Wilson's hypocrisy, African Americans proved to be a driving force in the war.

Jefferson County had long-simmering racial divides ever since the end of the Civil War. While racially driven violence and segregation typically associated with the Deep South was not as prevalent in Jefferson County, this does not mean that it didn't happen. Many communities in Jefferson County were legally segregated in some areas. Black citizens were not allowed to attend Shepherd College, as well as other public institutions in the county. In 1906, members of the Niagara Movement met in Harpers Ferry and marched around John Brown's Fort barefoot as a symbol that African Americans were still fighting for their rights. When in 1915 the Supreme Court ended the "grandfather clause" that was used to keep many African Americans from voting, the *Shepherdstown Register* noted:

> *This decision will, it is said, apply also to all of those southern states which after many years evolved plans to suppress this class of voters, and the way will be opened to give them the majority unless some new plan can be devised. It is simply impossible for the people of the south to tolerate the conditions that prevailed thirty or forty years ago, and some way will have to be found to maintain the supremacy of the white voters.*[102]

When the United States entered the First World War, many eyes turned to the African American community. Would black citizens support and fight for a country that seemingly had turned its back on them with institutionalized segregation in the Jim Crow South and the very military in which they would serve? For most, it was a belief that if they could prove themselves in war, then their social stature would be improved. As one African American teacher in the South put it, "[W]hen we have proved ourselves men, worthy to work and fight and die for our country, a grateful nation may gladly give us the recognition of real men, and the rights and privileges of true and loyal citizens."[103] These hopes were echoed by the National Association for the Advancement of Colored People (NAACP) and influential spokesperson W.E.B. Du Bois.[104] Secretary of the NAACP James W. Johnson even went as far as to say that "any man who was not willing to fight for his country was not worthy to be one of its citizens."[105]

The biggest problem facing the black community, however, was not black opposition to serving but white opposition to it. Whites feared the idea of arming and training African Americans in combat, for it "might lead to dangerous black militancy after the war."[106] Even when it came to noncombat personnel, African Americans were still discriminated against, as the army was in desperate need of doctors and dentists but African Americans in these professions were often turned down. Much to the dismay of the African American community, one argument of the United States government was to point out that black units would most likely be laborers rather than combat units, but this did little to quiet the worried white community. In August 1917, Chief of Staff Tasker Bliss offered six plans in dealing with how to employ black soldiers in the army—using black units as only service troops was the sixth plan. This plan ensured that at least 35 percent of black soldiers would be combat personnel; however, when put into practice, 80 percent of the troops were put on labor duty, with only 20 percent ever seeing combat.[107]

Jefferson County had more than 120 African Americans serve in World War I, making up an incredible 20 percent of the men who served from the county.[108] Despite this enthusiastic response to helping the war effort, African Americans still faced threats to their freedoms at home. In 1915, the popular Ku Klux Klan (KKK) recruiting tool, the film *The Birth of a Nation*, was released. The year 1915 was also the year racial violence began to resurface in the South—although not all of them were linked with the KKK, one hundred people were lynched that year.[109] In 1918, that very same film would make its way to the Shepherdstown Opera House. An advertisement for the film being shown on January 9 stated that it was "your last chance to see D.W. Griffith's gigantic military spectacle." With eighteen thousand people and three thousand horses, it is true that the film could be considered a spectacle at the time.[110] It is unclear whether the citizens knew what sort of spectacle they were in for, but they responded with great enthusiasm to see the film. An article noted:

> *Tickets for both performances are now on sale at the Opera House, and all who desire to see this wonderful story of the Southland should telephone or call for their seats without delay. The admission at the matinee will be 25c and 50c, while the night seats are selling at 25c, 50c, and 75c, with a few choice seats at $1.00. For the month of January this house has provided the strongest list of features ever shown.*[111]

Despite the setbacks their community faced, African Americans in Jefferson County still took pride in their service during the world war. One of the first African Americans to go overseas was a gentleman from Shepherdstown by the name of Daniel Stubbs, who was serving in the 505th Engineers Service Battalion. When Stubbs was about to leave the United States for France, he wrote a letter to his wife just before he boarded the justly named *President Lincoln* in which he stated:

> *I suppose you have been puzzled by not hearing from me for a long time, but it was not my fault. I could not help it. At this writing we are lying in harbor waiting for orders to sail for France, on a large transport, President Lincoln. There are 7,000 soldiers on this boat. We leave here tonight at 7:30 for France. Three transports leave together, carrying 30,000 soldiers for France. They will be surrounded by eighteen or twenty submarine chasers, torpedo boats, and battleships. When you get this letter you will know that we have arrived safe. We are all well. You won't receive mail from me very often on account of the long distance. Be of good cheer and take care of baby and yourself.*[112]

This letter was delayed by the censors to ensure that the news of the troop crossing did not fall into the wrong hands. Luckily, Stubbs made it across the Atlantic unharmed.

Little attention was paid to those members of the African American community who served in the military, and as a consequence, not much is known about them. In June 1918, a large draft class left Charles Town, and the sections of white and black draftees were segregated. The papers had long articles wishing the white troops luck in their adventures. But when it came to the African American troops, only a small paragraph was printed: "The twenty-eight colored men from this county drafted for army service entrained at Charles Town last Friday and left for Camp Sherman, Ohio. They were in charge of three of their number, Lincoln Jackson, John Adams, and Hite Lucas. A large crowd of colored persons was present to see them off."[113]

Although little attention was paid to the departure of these black troops, the press did update the public when they were found to have arrived safely to camp. Charlie Payne, one of the African American troops to leave with the draft class, wrote home that "the boys are all in good cheer" and that they "have [their] full outfits except the guns." Another trooper with this contingent was Alex Clark, who said that "when he gets among the Germans he means to take no prisoners—he just intends to kill 'em all."[114] Alex Clark was promoted to mess sergeant, and when he was asked if he liked the service, he replied, "Like it? I love it!"[115]

There was one case of an African American man from Jefferson County who found himself in trouble with the draft board. Arthur Johns was scheduled to appear before an examination with the draft board on a Tuesday morning in the summer of 1918; however, when the board adjourned that morning, pushing his examination back to the afternoon, Johns decided to leave. He told members of the board that "the government would have to pay him for the time he had lost in attending the examination." He was later arrested and sent to camp to be enrolled into the service.[116]

Few African Americans saw combat in France, but there were a few fatalities in the community. One was Edgar Skelton, who before leaving for the service married a woman by the name of Sadie Cliatic from Harpers Ferry. Edgar had entered service through being drafted on October 25, 1917. He died in France in April 1918, but it was unclear if it was from disease or combat. From the units that were in action at that time, it is likely that he died of disease.[117] Henry Washington was from Charles Town and was part of the 505th Engineers. He was drafted in the fall of 1917 and was killed in France in September 1918.[118] Martin Snyder was part of the 543rd Engineer Regiment. He died on October 12, 1918, and was buried at Plot A, Row 15, Grave 15 of the Suresnes American Cemetery, which is near Paris. Due to the location of his burial, it is likely that Snyder was a victim of disease or died of wounds received at the front.[119]

Although the African American experience was not well documented in Jefferson County, the story of African Americans in the First World War can also be told through Storer College. After the American Civil War ended, there was a large population of former slaves in Harpers Ferry, having followed the Union army. With this population came the need for education, since slaves had not been legally allowed to learn how to read or write. In the building now known as the Lockwood House, which had been used as General Philip Sheridan's headquarters in 1864, a small school was established for these former slaves. By 1867, thanks in part to a $10,000 donation from a New Englander by the name of John Storer, the small schoolhouse had become Storer College. The college did not discriminate based on race, religion or gender.

From these humble beginnings, Storer College began to expand into a sizable and well-respected educational institution. Almost every step of the way, however, the citizens of Harpers Ferry resisted the school that was growing on Camp Hill. Storer College teachers were pushed, spat on and had insults hurled at them in order to intimidate them into leaving. Although the town of Harpers Ferry had been a border town throughout the war, it seemed that the idea of African Americans being educated in their town was too much for some citizens. Despite the resistance, Storer continued to grow from that small schoolhouse to eventually having a small campus that included the old armory superintendent's house, which was renovated and expanded into Anthony Hall. This building was the centerpiece of the college, a massive building that held many classrooms and labs for student development.

Not far from Anthony Hall, a new building was added to Storer's campus: John Brown's Fort. This building was originally a fire engine house and guardsman room for the government's armory factory in lower town Harpers Ferry. It was made famous when, in 1859, John Brown used the building as a base of operations during his raid on the armory and arsenal. Brown made his final stand in the building and was knocked unconscious inside it and captured. Following the Civil War, the building was moved to Chicago to be part of the world's fair. There the building sat for several years until a fierce letter-writing and fundraising campaign brought the building

View of the staircase in the Storer College museum in the John Brown fort. Notice the sign that reads, "Contribute to Storer College in the memory of John Brown." Post–World War I. *Library of Congress.*

back to Harpers Ferry, but not to the same location where it had been. The closest piece of land that could be secured for the building was the Murphey Farm, two miles away from its original location. It was on this land that members of the Niagara Movement (predecessor to the NAACP), led by W.E.B. Du Bois, marched around the building with their shoes off in 1906. In 1911, the building was once again moved, this time to the campus of Storer College. The movement was symbolic—to have the building where

John Brown was captured and eventually executed for attempting to fight for the rights of African Americans on the campus of an all-black college. Even more symbolically, the interior of the building was turned into a museum dedicated to the history of African Americans. It stored several items, including chains and whips from the times of slavery.

When the United States entered the war in 1917, many Storer College students and alumni enthusiastically signed up to do their part. The president of the college at the time was Henry T. McDonald, who would become the longest-serving and most storied president the college ever had. McDonald did his best to ensure that diligent records were kept of the Storer boys who did their part in the war. He wrote to the men requesting that they respond with whatever service they were doing, as well as a picture of themselves in uniform. By McDonald's own count, 104 sons of Storer served in the armed forces in World War I; 102 of these men were in the army, and 2 of them were in the navy.[120]

One act that became very common during the Great War was for students serving overseas to send back souvenirs to the school. The objects usually had some sort of significance to the battles taking place in France and would become prized possessions of the school. In one instance, Dr. Paul V. Diggs "brought a piece of shrapnel and two machinegun bullets for the school."[121] Edward Snively was able to get a piece of a spring from a German airplane sent to the school. In his description of the object, he said, "The small piece of iron is a piece of a cylinder spring off a German aeroplane which was brought into our salvage dump. Four of us divided the whole spring up between us. Getting it cost us a few hours a piece on the wood pile."[122] McGlenard Williamson sent Storer College several items, including "a French prayer book, containing most interesting keepsakes of one who more than fifty years ago partook of her first communion; a copy of the Paris edition of the New York Herald; a small German joke book, whose jibes were especially aimed at

View of the Storer College museum located within the John Brown fort from the second floor. This is where many of the items soldiers sent to Henry T. McDonald and the school would end up on display. Post–World War I. *Library of Congress.*

Paul V.Diggs-Corporal

Above: A German World War I helmet sent to Storer College from Robert G. Green, a former student serving overseas. *Harpers Ferry National Historical Park.*

Opposite: Dr. Paul Diggs. *Harpers Ferry National Historical Park and West Virginia and Regional History Center, WVU Libraries.*

the French, and a German newspaper, which in size and quality of paper is an eloquent reminder for all time, of the straits into which the Central Powers were being driven."[123] One of the most coveted items obtained by Storer College during this time was a silver letter opener. The item came from George C. Blue, who was the husband of Mabel Beasley Blue, a Storer graduate, class of 1911. The letter opener obtained by Mr. Blue was taken from the house that the crown prince of Germany used as his living quarters while on the Alsace-Lorraine front in the war and was "doubtless used by him."[124] All these objects were put on display in the museum within John Brown's Fort.

Perhaps the most popular item sent back to Storer College were helmets. Those soldiers who were on the front lines went out of their way to get German helmets to send home to be put on display. Robert G. Green sent a German helmet to his alma mater that was described as "a source of wonderment for many, in that it is such a big heavy thing. One might think it large enough for an atlas to wear."[125] Another similarly named student, Robert P. Green, stated in a letter, "I sent you a German helmet, I hope you received it alright. I will send you something else if I can get it."[126] Fred Morris was serving overseas and reported that when he returned home, he would stop by Storer to deliver one of his two German officer helmets to the school's museum. Clarence T. Napper sent a helmet that was described as follows:

> *Another carefully packed helmet came from Sergt. Clarence T. Napper. This too was one captured from a German, or left by him when he went "west" or somewhere else. It showed service. As an object of interest in the museum it will serve a much more humanitarian purpose than it did when it was worn by one who would destroy civilization.*[127]

Edgar Snively, who presented the school with the piece of German airplane, also sent Storer a "Boche" helmet for the museum. All the items that McGlenard Williamson had sent to the school came wrapped inside a German helmet as well. Frederick Wims changed things up, however, and sent Storer a blue French helmet that came "with a small French tri-color attached to it, it has been an object of interest to many, while it rested on the chapel piano."[128] All the items sent to Storer College from its sons were irrefutable evidence that Storer had done its part in supporting the United States in the Great War.

Clarence T. Napper. *Harpers Ferry National Historical Park and West Virginia and Regional History Center, WVU Libraries.*

Perhaps even more compelling than the objects sent to Storer College were the letters that the soldier boys sent to President McDonald. These letters detailed the heartfelt fondness these men felt for Storer, as well as described the vast horrors of war that they saw over there. To summarize these letters would be a great injustice to the men who wrote

Unidentified Storer College student in navy uniform. *Harpers Ferry National Historical Park and West Virginia and Regional History Center, WVU Libraries.*

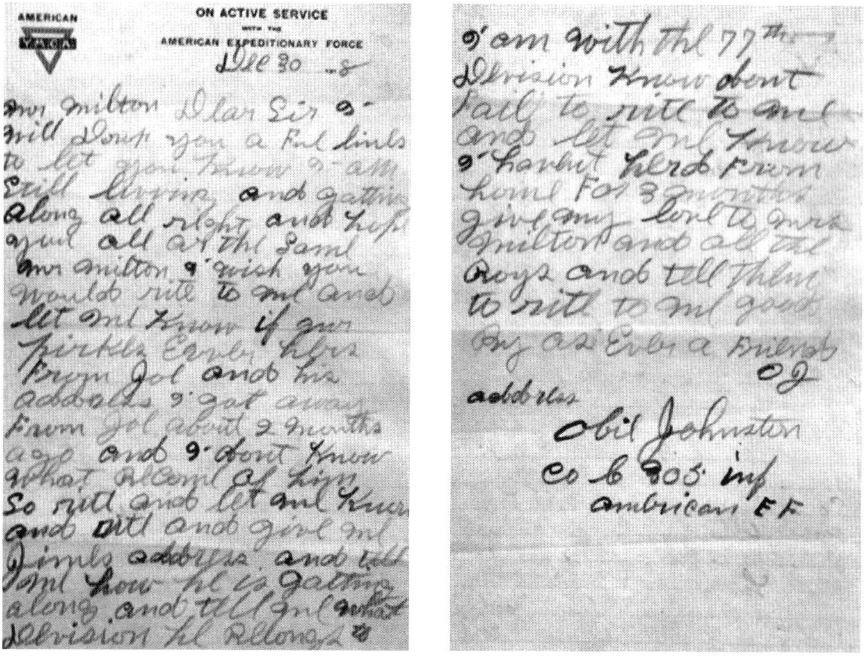

AMERICAN Y.M.C.A.
ON ACTIVE SERVICE WITH THE AMERICAN EXPEDITIONARY FORCE
Dec 30 -8

mr milton Dear Sir I will drop you a few lines to let you know I am still living and getting along all right and hope you all are the same mr milton I wish you would rite to me and let me know if our Pirkle Early hears from Joe and his address I got away from Joe about 2 months ago and I dont know what become of him So rite and let me know and rite and give me Jimmy address and tell me how he is getting along and tell me what division he belongs to

I am with the 77th Division know dont fail to rite to me and let me know I havent heard from home for 3 months give my love to mrs milton and all the Boys and tell them to rite to me good by as Ever a friend OJ

address
Obie Johnston
Co C 305 inf
american EF

Wartime letter from Obie Johnston. *Jefferson County Historical Society.*

them, for the power they hold could not be properly conveyed (although they will be edited for length).

Robert P. Green wrote the following letter of his experiences in the 808th Pioneer Infantry Regiment, Medical Corps, AEF:

> *I am glad that I was physically fit for the service, although I have had it tough at times, but that was not long, but I took that like a man and looked forward to the future, for I realize the road to success is not smooth. I have had the opportunity to see the ruin and utter devastation wrought by the cursed Huns in their inroads on France. I have been in the Verdun and Argonne sector ever since I have been over here. We landed in the Argonne Forest on Sept. 20th, a few days before the drive started. I was under shell fire from the 26th of Sept. until the armistice was signed. My gas mask which was my friend, I kept at an alert position at all times, day and night, also my helmet and other necessary things. I will not try to tell my experiences in this letter for I could not do justice to you and myself. I have seen with my own eyes some of the gothic piles, those that remain in the sector where I am, most of which have been damaged.…I have found the*

> *French to be a warm hearted and grateful people. They put forth every effort to make it pleasant for a soldier, I know this to be true from contact.*[129]

Anthony Y. Lewis entered service with the 505th Engineer Corps and provided service in building railroads and other infrastructure projects in France. He wrote this letter to President McDonald following the armistice:

> *Just a few lines to let you know that I am well and getting along as well as ever. One year ago today we first saw the coast of France and at nine o'clock in the morning we dropped anchor at Breast, Dec. 27th, 1918. Man, many things have happened since then, but I am glad to say that I have passed through all, and can say I was here to watch the American Expeditionary Forces grow from infancy to a full grown man.…My health has been excellent since I have been here, I have only been sick once and then it was mumps and of course I could not keep from getting them when so great a number of the company had them. I used to have the tonsillitis often when I was in the states but I have only had one light attack of it since I have been here.…I have, as everyone should have, a clean record in my company. I have never been brought up before any of my officers for a reprimand. Christmas this year was not so good as it could have been, yet it could have been worse. I am certain that it was the happiest one that thousands of people over here had celebrated for quite a while. I know that had not the war ended when it did our Christmas would have been much different to what it was. Then we have something to be thankful for.*[130]

Gouveneur M. Page graduated from Storer College in 1908, and when the United States entered the First World War, he ended up joining the 803rd Infantry Regiment. Just a little over a month after the armistice was signed, he penned a letter to President McDonald:

> *I am sure Storer contributed generously in men to the army showing in a true way her liberal and mighty spirit. I have been fortunate enough to run across a few of the Storer boys who were attached to various organizations. It would be useless for me to attempt, in a letter to narrate where I have been, what I have seen or my experience in France. No doubt you have followed the events of the war closely in the papers, and celebrated its termination with thanks to the Almighty. However carefully one may have read, it would be, and is almost impossible to draw a picture from their imagination of the terrible destruction wrought by the bloodiest of bloody*

Left: Anthony Y. Lewis. *Harpers Ferry National Historical Park and West Virginia and Regional History Center, WVU Libraries.*

Below: Envelope from a soldier in camp. *Jefferson County Historical Society.*

conflicts. Now since it has ceased and the guns are as monsters asleep, I hope to soon return to the States and shall try at an early date to once again visit Old Storer. If it should be my good fortune to visit the "Home of the Old Gold" I shall try to interest you more with a verbal description than I can in a letter....I have no idea when we leave for the States, and am

> *staying at present in dugouts left by the Germans, near St. Mihiel. This is on the Verdun front. They built them as if they intended to stay but Uncle Sam's boys came over and drove them away.*[131]

Henry C. Ridgely shared with McDonald his feelings of great pride from participating in the Great War. While serving in France, Ridgely came in contact with many French citizens and began to notice a stark difference from those in the United States:

> *Now that the war is practically over the hope of everyone is to return home. Indeed the French people are the most freedom loving people in the world. They have been rejoicing and celebrating since the signing of the Armistice. The American soldiers are also rejoiced and happy over their victory, yet many of them wept because they would not be allowed to destroy Germany after the manner which the Germans destroyed France. To have been a soldier in the World War is one of the greatest blessings fortune could have given to mankind, yet countless souls have been swallowed in death. But when we think of the World Peace which will soon flood the Universe forever, surely those men that gave their lives so nobly and earnestly have not died in vain. The one thing for which the French people will be ever remembered is that they show no prejudice toward a man because of his color, if you* [are] *capable they readily give you the right away; in other words they say "A Man is a Man for A' That." The social life here is so different from that of the States; here, if one is a gentleman and with an appreciative amount of culture you can go anywhere and associate with any of these people so long as you play the part of a man. The French people indeed were unfamiliar in no sense with colored troops for they have millions of their own. The color of the French soldiers is the only way you can distinguish one from the other, because it is certainly no difference in social life....I have not mentioned any of the horrors of war because I feel that you are tired from reading concerning such.*[132]

The differences that Henry Ridgely saw in the French society were not unique to his experience. While colored units were serving in France, treatment by the French concerned many white American officers, who became worried as to how these soldiers would react upon returning home, especially in the Jim Crow South. This worried the military so much that Colonel J.A. Linard, head of the French Military Mission attached to the United States, released a memo to French officers and civilians to not "spoil" African American troops because it would damage American and French relations. The French General Staff quickly repudiated the remarks by Linard, which made the American military look foolish as far as race relations were concerned. Linard even went as far as to say that no intimacy other than civil politeness should be observed between white and black troops or civilians. This incident would be just a small taste of tensions between the United States and France when it came to how each dealt with the issue of race.[133]

Clarence I. Upper was one of the last soldiers to respond to Henry T. McDonald's call for letters about their service. In his letter, he talks about the great misdeeds that he witnessed in Europe and how fortunate citizens of the United States should feel:

> *It was newsy and strong in determination to bring the Hun to strict accountability for his ravage on civilization in general and France and Belgium in particular, too much cannot be said about the cruelties of the Germans imposed upon innocent women and children. To my thinking this is the saddest chapter of the war, disrespect and degeneration of womanhood and the heavy toll and burden placed on childhood living and potential. Every nation in my opinion should be judged or condemned in proportion as it regards and protects its weakest members, womanhood and childhood. The American people can not possibly know and realize conditions as they exist in this part of the world, "things seen are greater than the things heard of." I would love to give my impressions more fully what I have seen and experienced, but being a soldier I must write simply as a soldier, but I hope on my return to be able to teach thereby giving hundreds the benefits of knowledge and experience I gained over here....* [Y]*es I know my own people much better since I have had a chance to compare them with other peoples for, without exaggeration I think I have seen every race and nationality and have some idea of their customs and conditions....I can not express my feeling in words when the name of Storer College is mentioned. She has done so much for me that the only hope of repaying her is to try and live a clean and upright life, a life that will never bring reproach to her fair name. I realize more every day how much I owe to my ideal home training and the heightening and wholesome influence I was taught at Storer, when I see hundreds of my companions less fortunate than I.*[134]

Two soldiers from Storer College who had rather unique experiences when it came to the war were Robert A. McNeal (class of 1908) and

Douglass Freeman. *Harpers Ferry National Historical Park and West Virginia Regional History Center, WVU Libraries.*

Maurice Reid (class of 1914). These two men served in the 351st Field Artillery, 93rd Division. What makes their experiences so unique is that the 93rd Division is one of only two African American divisions that actually were on the front lines of combat in the First World War. McNeal and Reid were right in the thick of fighting, with their largest action coming in the Meuse-Argonne Offensive. The division was so proud of its service that its division patch paid homage to its predecessors with an image of a buffalo, in reference to the famous Buffalo Soldiers who came before them.[135]

Only one of Storer's boys lost his life during the world war. John Tindley was serving at the rank of sergeant in Company K, 813th Pioneer Infantry Regiment. While serving in France, Sergeant Tindley became ill and succumbed to pneumonia on October 3, 1918. Storer said of him that he was "the one Storer boy for whom a gold star will always shine in our service flag."[136] Today, John Tindley is buried in Plot C, Row 3, Grave 12 at the Oise-Aisne American Cemetery.[137]

When the AEF returned from France in 1919, a specific group became the target of racial violence: African American World War I veterans. In the summer of 1919, scores of African Americans were brutally massacred and huge race riots erupted in the North, thus giving the time its nickname "Red Summer."[138] Much of the violence directly targeted black soldiers. At least ten of the lynching victims of 1919 were black veterans, some even still in uniform.[139] In one Georgia incident, a black soldier by the name of Daniel Mack claimed that he had fought in France and would not take the mistreatment at home. He was then sentenced to jail for thirty days but was later taken from his cell and beaten to death by an angry mob.[140] In another case, a veteran was killed by a mob simply for not getting off the sidewalk for a white woman.[141]

While lynching was a traditional form of racial violence, this year saw the emergence of burning victims alive—at least eleven documented

Above: Unidentified Storer College student in uniform. *Harpers Ferry National Historical Park and West Virginia Regional History Center, WVU Libraries.*

Opposite: Forest Griffin Johnson. *Harpers Ferry National Historical Park and West Virginia and Regional History Center, WVU Libraries.*

cases.[142] The summer of 1919 also saw an explosion of race riots, the worst in Washington, D.C., Chicago and Omaha but many more in cities both north and south.[143] While many are unsure of the underlying cause of the riots, the return of the black soldiers does appear to be the trigger. Many white papers such as the *Current Opinion* and *Time* magazine even claimed that black citizens had turned violent due to their war experiences and training.[144]

When it came to African Americans fighting back against oppression upon the AEF's return from France, W.E.B. Du Bois famously said in the NAACP magazine, *Crisis*, "We return. We return from fighting. We return fighting. Make way for democracy!"[145] This illustrates how the First World War was a turning point for African Americans. Instead of just rolling over and allowing whites to trample their rights, they began to fight back. It should be noted that in the race riots of the Red Summer of 1919, many black citizens did fight back, using firearms to defend themselves and their property.[146] The *New York World* noticed the difference and, attributing it to the return of black soldiers, asked:

> *Who is foolish enough to assume that with 239,000 colored men in uniform from the southern states alone, as against 370,000 white men, the blacks whose manhood and patriotism were thus recognized and tested are forever to be flogged, lynched, burned at the stake or chased into concealment whenever Caucasian desperadoes are moved to engage in this infamous past time?*[147]

It was just that, though. The African American community had proven its patriotism in the war and was not going to simply accept large-scale white violence without fighting back. The white violence was also mixed with the fact that many of the goals and aims of the African American community

going into the war had not been achieved, such as racial equality and the end of Jim Crow. Alain Locke, an outspoken progressive black leader, expressed the disappointment, stating:

> *The anticipated rewards of the Negro's patriotic response to the idealism of the "War to Save Democracy" were not measurably realized and, spurred by the bitter disillusionments of post-war indifference there came that desperate intensification of the Negro's race consciousness and attempt at recovery of group morale.*[148]

Furthermore, lynching was still not considered a violation of federal law, nor had the Wilson administration truly attempted to recognize lynching as an issue. At one point, Wilson did state that it was difficult to advocate democracy during the war if America could not protect its weak, but this only pointed out his own contradictions.[149] It was clear to many that violence as retaliation or defense would not be enough to achieve equality

Left: Edward Dickerson. *Harpers Ferry National Historical Park and West Virginia and Regional History Center, WVU Libraries.*

Right: Thomas E. Busby. *Harpers Ferry National Historical Park and West Virginia and Regional History Center, WVU Libraries.*

Above: The entrance gates to Storer College, dedicated to Storer College students who fought in "the World War." *Library of Congress.*

Left: Thomas E. Busby in camp. *Harpers Ferry National Historical Park and West Virginia Regional History Center, WVU Libraries.*

and that other attempts to reach out to the government and the public had to be made.

The effects of the pride rightfully gained in the African American community following the world war were even starting to be felt on the Storer College campus. President Henry T. McDonald hinted in his annual report that there had been some trouble with students during the 1919–20 school year. It appears that students were looking to have a voice in the decisions made at Storer. These tensions culminated in a student strike in November 1922. McDonald said of this strike, "[T]he restive feeling which has taken hold of so many of the schools for colored youth and manifested itself in so many and varied ways, finally came to an unexpected and unwelcome head here in November." While unclear what preceded the protests, the end result was the expulsion of three students and disciplinary action for several others.[150]

When Thomas Busby returned from service, he, like many other Storer students, was very proud of the good work that African American soldiers had provided during the war. As he looked at what the future had in store for the community, he offered a small poem, "Yesterday," in which he wrote:

Today the shadows fall across our path,
Our stony path, that winds uphill all the way;
We stumble on the blindness—God be praised,
No one can rob us of our yesterday.

"Tomorrow, oh tomorrow, who can tell
What joy or sorrow may be ours?" we say;
We stumble on in blindness—God be praised,
No one can rob us of our yesterday.[151]

The civil rights movement sparked by the world war continues even to this day. Storer College, on the other hand, does not. Following the *Brown v. Board of Education of Topeka* Supreme Court case in 1954, in which it was found that segregation in schools was unconstitutional, Storer rapidly lost enrollment and eventually state funding. In 1955, the college closed its doors. Today, the campus is owned by the National Park Service. The gates to Storer College still exist on the campus, and they remain a memorial to the First World War. On the left side of the gate, a concrete slab reads, "To the Students of Storer College who fought in the Civil War 1861–1865, Spanish American War 1898, The World War 1917–1918." The other side reads, "May their illustrious example inspire us to a loyal sense of duty to our country."

Chapter 5

CHARLES TOWN

In 1780, a gentleman by the name of Charles Washington moved out toward what is now known as Jefferson County. At the time, Charles's brother, George, was in the midst of leading the fight to make a new country. However, it is believed that George, who had previously scouted the area for a company as a young adult, suggested to Charles to move out to this region. After having established his homestead, Happy Retreat, Charles petitioned to have the area incorporated into Charlestown (later Charles Town), which was granted in 1786. The main roads in town were named after family members, such as George, and the main drag in town would be Washington Street. It was Charles's deep wish that the main purpose of Washington Street be for the use of public buildings. With this in mind, in 1803, the courthouse was completed at the center of the town. It was then that Charles Town became the county seat of Jefferson County, Virginia.[152]

In 1859, when John Brown launched his raid on the United States Arsenal and Armory in Harpers Ferry, several militia members from Charles Town answered the call to help suppress the potential slave insurrection. Brown had also taken captive the grandson of Charles Washington and great-grandnephew of George Washington, Colonel Lewis Washington. When the U.S. marines stormed the engine house and captured John Brown and several other raiders, they were handed over to Virginia authorities. From there the raiders were sent to Charles Town to await trial at the county seat, staying in the jail just across the street from the courthouse (the modern-day post office). Charles Town had suddenly been put on the national stage, and the eyes of the country were fixed on the town. For safety reasons, Virginia militia and cadets from the Virginia Military Institute guarded the town, which was placed under martial law and curfews, all in fear of some abolitionist force attacking the town to free Brown and the other raiders.

Brown and the raiders were charged with three crimes: murder, treason and inciting slave rebellion. The raiders were found guilty and sentenced to be hanged to death.[153] The decision enraged a large part of the country and further divided the nation. Brown was hanged a month after his trial just outside town, and the other raiders were hanged in the jailhouse yard. The further division of the nation from the fallout of John Brown's trial in Charles Town ultimately helped lead to the start of the American Civil War, which began just sixteen months after Brown's execution.

During the Civil War, Charles Town found itself, like the rest of Jefferson County, right in the midst of the fighting. Several small battles took place in and around the town. Through this the town faced a lot of destruction, including the destabilization of the famous courthouse, which had sustained brutal artillery fire. When the war ended, the courthouse was far too unstable, so the county seat was temporarily moved to Shepherdstown. In the meantime, Charles Town worked to restore and stabilize its historic building, and upon completion, the county seat left Shepherdstown and returned to the Charles Town Courthouse, where it remains today. After the county seat had returned to Charles Town, the town underwent a seemingly massive expansion. More and more people moved to Charles Town, building large Victorian-style homes and expanding the town limits even past the fields where John Brown had been hanged just years before.[154]

When the Great War started in Europe in 1914, many people in Charles Town, as well as the rest of Jefferson County, would have skimmed over articles that described the battles and horrors occurring so far away. While it is unclear whether these articles drew much attention from the readers, it is important to note that articles likely had an influence over Americans' view of the war. When the war started, a great interest was shown in the tactics being used on the battlefield. It is likely that the Civil War veterans within Jefferson County were interested to see how war had changed in the past fifty years. One article explored the use of field artillery:

> *The object of field artillery is to support the infantry in its advances or its retreats. It aims to hit the part of the enemy which is most dangerous to the friendly infantry and which would hinder its success. Since the enemy's artillery would do the same thing, it is evident that a modern battle will*

> *generally begin with an artillery duel, and that whichever side is able to silence the other side's artillery will have a tremendous advantage.*[155]

When the armies in Europe became stalemated on the Western Front and trench warfare became the norm, readers became interested in how exactly trench warfare worked. Although words cannot accurately depict the horrors of trench warfare, one Jefferson County reporter received accounts of the battles and tried:

> *The so-called Battle of the Aisne was a siege rather than a battle; it resembled the operations round Richmond or Vicksburg rather than the engagements at Gettysburg or Antietam. For weeks and even months the soldiers of both armies lived in the cleverly constructed trenches they had dug among the hills and stone quarries.... Ten days! Aeroplanes watching us, and shells flying overhead by day, alarms and rifle fire by night. We live the life of a rabbit, digging ourselves deeper and deeper into the earth, until we are completely sheltered from above, coming out now and then, when things are quiet to cook and eat.*[156]

Even worse news came from the European front in 1915 when the belligerent nations began using a new weapon: gas. The introduction of chemical warfare brought a whole new level of horror to the First World War, as well as to the eyes of readers in Charles Town:

> *When the shell explodes the gases caused by the explosion spread over the ground in a circle having a diameter of about 100 yards. The gases produce paralyses of some of the vital organs of the body, with the result that every living thing within this circle is killed instantly and painlessly, and so far as is now known there is no defense against nor antidote for the action of these gases.*[157]

As the war continued, many in Jefferson County wondered how the European war had gotten to the point it was at, with the allies seemingly just barely hanging on and both sides having to dig in. The reporters in the county went back to the power of the German war machine:

> *Whatever the outcome of the war, and whatever opinions we may hold of the effectiveness of the German Army as a body of fighting men, there is no question that in the preparation and mobilization the German machine*

> *moved with all the smoothness and accuracy that its admirers had expected it to show....The result of this inevitably efficient organization was rapid advance through Belgium and northern France that almost reached the wall of Paris within a month.*[158]

Despite the cause, all could agree that the results were horrible. And the people of Jefferson County received many reports showing what a terrible meat grinder the First World War was turning out to be:

> *The European nations now at war have lost 5,950,000 men in the first eight months of 'the conflict, and spent $8,400,000,000 in the first six months, according to figures prepared for the Avanti, a socialist newspaper in Rome, by its military expert...a loss equal to that of the European war would wipe out every male inhabitant between the ages of eighteen and forty-five years in the District of Columbia and the states of Maryland, Virginia, Maine, New Hampshire, Vermont, Massachusetts, Rhode Island, Connecticut, New York, New Jersey, Pennsylvania and Delaware.*[159]

With such horrible reports readily available to the people of Jefferson County and the rest of the United States, the question arose: if America were to enter the First World War, would there be enough volunteers to make the American military an effective fighting force? We may never know the answer to this question, as within a month of Congress declaring war on Germany and the Central Powers, President Woodrow Wilson had put a bill before Congress urging it to issue a draft.

The Selective Service Act of 1917 had several parameters to which the citizens of Charles Town paid close attention. For one, the governors of the states would appoint county sheriffs as registrars for the draft in order to take names of men between the ages of nineteen and twenty-five who are

Jefferson County native Frank Bane (*left*) with a companion in their World War I uniforms. *Jefferson County Historical Society.*

Left: Photo of Noel Burton, a Jefferson County native, in uniform. 1918. *Jefferson County Historical Society.*

Below: World War I draftees with Dr. Neil (*left*) and Captain Jack Getzendanner (*right*) in 1918. *Jefferson County Historical Society.*

eligible to be drafted—any man unwilling to register for the draft would be arrested. Several people would be exempt from military service, however, such as state officers, persons engaged in industries found to be necessary to the maintenance of the military establishment and those men who worked in agricultural industries necessary for food production. It was estimated that this bill led to the enrollment of 7 million men, with about 40 percent being weeded out on account of disabilities; the rest would be subject to being drafted into the armed forces.[160]

When the Selective Service Act was passed, Governor John J. Cornwell released a statement to the citizens of West Virginia:

> *The regularly appointed registrars in each precinct will be delegated to act as enrolling officers. The enrollment cards and registration certificates will be sent direct from the War Department to the sheriff of each county, and the registrars must obtain them from the sheriffs before the day named by the President in his proclamation. In each county there will be created a board of military census and enrollment composed of the sheriff, the county clerk, a physician and one citizen from each of the dominant political parties. This board will supervise the enrollment and eliminate from the list those who will be excluded under the law and the President's proclamation because of physical disability or for other reasons named in the act of Congress.*[161]

In accordance with the orders that Governor Cornwell gave to the state of West Virginia, the draft offices for Jefferson County would be placed in Charles Town. The conscription board in Jefferson County was made up of the following members: Sheriff Charles T. Engle, County Clerk Charles A. Johnson, County Health Officer Dr. J.M. Miller, J. William Rider and Captain H.C. Getzendanner. These men had one of the most important roles in Jefferson County during the First World War. They had the power to select from an estimated 1,588 eligible men from the county and decide who was fit to go to war. Sheriff Charles T. Engle released a statement to the governor in which he said, "[The] board sits Thursday. All registrars summoned to be present to receive instructions and supplies. Jefferson County can be counted on to respond faithfully and patriotically to the proclamation."[162] It is no surprise that with such an important task at hand and so many lives at stake, political differences occurred regarding the draft board. The biggest outcry came from the town of Shepherdstown, which released a statement:

> *Some regret has been expressed that there is no representative of Shepherdstown or Shepherdstown district on the Jefferson County board of conscription. Of the five members of the board who have been designated to make the selection of soldiers to constitute Jefferson County's quota for the draft, four are from Charles Town, the fifth being of the Harpers Ferry district. It is not a position which anyone desires, and we know of no one who would like to have it, but it might have been better to have had the representation more general.*[163]

Despite the protests of Shepherdstown as far as the makeup of the draft board, the men still convened in Charles Town to complete their task. Draft registration cards were distributed asking men to fill out information, including their name, date of birth, employment and whether they claimed any exemption from military service.[164] Men who registered with the draft board were separated into five different classes. Class 5 were men who were ineligible for military service, perhaps based on having an occupation in the government, being a member of the clergy or being someone who was deemed medically unfit for service. Class 4 were men who were depended on as the sole provider of their household. Class 3 and Class 2 registrants were men who were temporarily unavailable for military service for a varying degree of reasons. And Class 1 registrants were men who were eligible and liable for military service. When draft selections were made, they would most likely come from the Class 1 category.

Several calls for draft classes, both big and small, occurred all throughout America's involvement in the First World War. In January 1918, a call was made for Class 1 men to enter the service, and figures indicated that at that time there was a pool of 1 million men in the United States who could be drafted under this call. Provost Marshal General Crowder of the United States assured the public that the drafting would be evenly distributed among the states.[165] After this call was made, many of the Jefferson County men who had exemptions waived those claims, signifying their willingness to serve their country.[166] While many men were willing to serve, some in the public of Jefferson County feared what it would mean for their workforce. The *Charles Town Advocate*, for instance, had reason to be concerned when the call came:

> *The selective service law has hit the Advocate office an awful blow. All three of the young men employed in the office have been caught in the draft net. Glen C. Fleming, printer and press feeder, and John W. Gore, job printer, have already been placed in Class 1, while Brown L. Rissler, our*

> *machine operator, is a safe bet for a position in the same class, as he has made no claim to exemption, although his classification has not yet been made. With these three men in France, or on the way there, the remainder of the working force, that means "us," will have to take an enforced vacation. Is there a farmer anywhere in the county in need of an orphan for adoption until the cruel war is over?*[167]

In February 1918, the Jefferson County Exemption and Enrollment Board began working toward Jefferson County's quota for the upcoming draft class—185 men who were placed in the Class 1 classification were brought to Charles Town to be physically examined to determine if they were fit for service.[168] During this process, the board was proud to announce that of the 1,100 eligible men for registration in Jefferson County, only 21 did not return their draft questionnaires. The county also boasted that during the whole registration process, many of the officials did not receive pay for their work, making the total cost for the county to register draft-eligible men about $124, plus $50 paid to the clerk.[169]

One way that Jefferson County was able to fulfill its draft quotas was by deducting the number of men in the county who volunteered for service from the number of men needing to be drafted to fulfill the quota. In the February draft class, 32 Jefferson County men had enthusiastically decided to volunteer for military service. This left the quota needed for that class to be filled at 104 men. In this draft, the papers also printed lists of men who

Seven limited-service World War I draftees, with Dr. Neil (*left*) and Captain Jack Getzendanner (*right*). 1918. *Jefferson County Historical Society.*

were denied for service due to physical requirements, showing that truly no one had any sense of privacy during the First World War.[170] This process of issuing a call for drafted men, followed by quotas being distributed from the states, which then issued quotas to the counties or regions to fill, would continue throughout the entire war, even through the armistice. All in all, it is difficult to decipher just how many men from Jefferson County who served in the Great War were drafted, but doubtless it is a large portion of the more than 530 men who served. When these men were sent off to camp, they were usually sent off with a celebration by locals in Charles Town, who met them at the railroad station in town. The scene of one of these sendoffs was described by the *Shepherdstown Register*:

> *Sixty-one young men from Jefferson County left Charles Town yesterday evening for Camp Lee to go into training for the army service. It was the largest contingent that has yet been called, and was composed of a fine body of young fellows. The men assembled at 2.30, when they were received by Captain H.C. Getzendanner, chairman of the local board, and given their instructions. Later in the afternoon the women of Charles Town entertained them at a bountiful lunch in the firemen's hall, treating them delightfully, and the Red Cross presented each man with a sweater and a package of useful articles....At 6 o'clock the party headed by two bands, marched to the B&O station where an immense crowd had assembled to see them off. The bands played spirited music continuously but there was a sadness among the friends and relatives that could not be dispelled, and many tears were shed.*[171]

Of course, Charles Town, like the other towns in Jefferson County, was very proud of its soldier boys who went overseas in the First World War. The town kept close track of these boys, reporting on their movements and any news heard of them. One of the proudest moments Charles Town experienced was not due to an American soldier, but rather a soldier in the British army. Lieutenant George Alexander Porterfield Jr. was the grandson of Colonel George A. Porterfield, who was a resident in Charles Town. Lieutenant Porterfield was serving in a Worcestershire regiment in the British Expeditionary Forces in France and was to be awarded the military cross for gallant conduct during the fighting in Flanders (likely the Battle of Passchendaele):

> *The military cross is one of three most highly prized decorations in the British army. In addition to its character as a badge of courageous*

World War I draftees in front of the Getzendanner House on Washington Street. 1918. *Jefferson County Historical Society.*

> *achievement, it carries also the attraction of ceremonies investiture when the King in person makes the presentation. The investiture in the case of Lieutenant Porterfield will take place at Buckingham Palace, some time in the current month.*[172]

Another Jefferson County boy who served in a foreign military was Clarence Wood. Wood had entered the Canadian Expeditionary Forces in September 1915 and made his way to France. In 1918, Wood was captured and taken prisoner by the Germans. He wrote to his mother from a prison camp deep in the heart of Germany:

> *You remember what a bookworm I used to be. I have lots of time to read now. I have studied French and Spanish for some time, and you can judge how I occupy my time. We also knit gloves, socks, and sweaters to pass the time away. Give my best regards to all the folks and KEEP SMILING.*[173]

Many people in Charles Town kept their eyes on casualty lists to see if any locals had been hit in the fighting abroad, and there were a few. Major

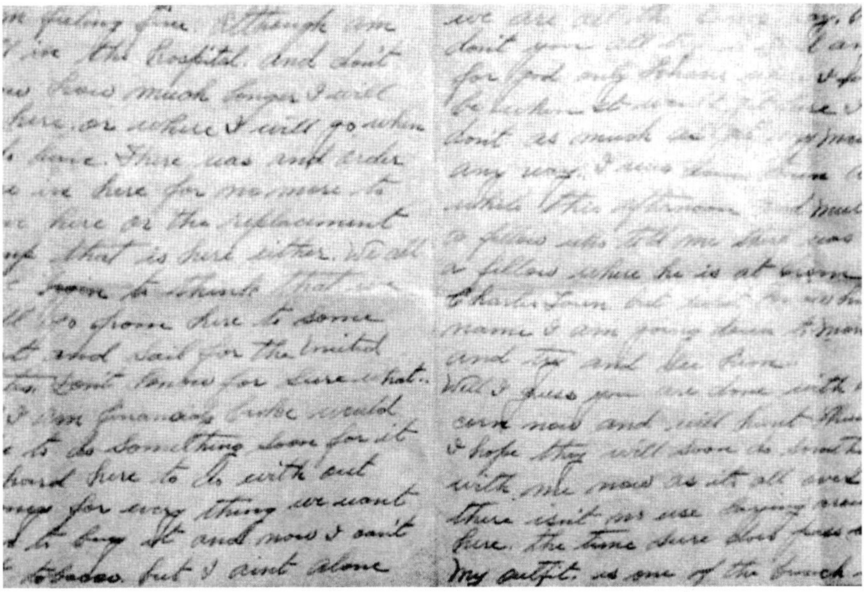

Letter from James W. Milton to his father after the war. *Jefferson County Historical Society.*

Battery A of the 313th Field Artillery. *Jefferson County Historical Society.*

Above: Holiday postcard from a soldier in camp. *Jefferson County Historical Society.*

Right: James W. Milton. *Jefferson County Historical Society.*

J.P. Lucas had married Miss Wynkopp of Charles Town before he went off to war. While serving in France, he received a gunshot wound to the head, causing a fractured skull. He was, however, able to survive the wounding and progressed enough that he soon was able to write a letter to his wife letting her know that he was okay.[174] Ervin Chamberlin was a Charles Town boy who was wounded in the summer of 1918, although there are no details as to what his wound was.[175] George W. Jones had enlisted in the engineers shortly after the United States entered the Great War. He had previously mentioned in a letter that he was seeing some pretty heavy fighting. In September 1918, he was reported as having been wounded, but the degree of his wound is not known.[176]

James Milton was a local of Jefferson County living not far outside Charles Town. Milton joined the 313th Field Artillery, a unit that many in Jefferson County followed due to a high volume of Jefferson County boys in the unit. The *Shepherdstown Register* reported in February 1918 that regiments of the 313th, 314th and 315th Field Artilleries of the 80th Division were mostly West Virginia men, with most of the drafted Jefferson County boys going to the 313th. Milton's experiences in the 313th are well documented, as he wrote to his parents and sweetheart almost every day of the war. There was much rejoicing in Jefferson County when in June 1918 word had been received that the 313th had made it to France safely. However, Milton did not stay with the 313th. He ended up transferring to the 30th Infantry regiment of the 3rd Division, known as the "Rock of the Marne." While serving, James

Left: James W. Milton and a friend in camp. *Jefferson County Historical Society*.

Below: A group of World War I veterans on Washington Street by the office of Dr. James Ranson Jr. These veterans were the original group that created the Jackson Perks post of the American Legion. *Jefferson County Historical Society*.

Milton was severely gassed and had to be hospitalized. From the hospital, he wrote to his father after the war ended:

> *I am feeling fine, although I am still in the hospital, and I don't know how much longer I will be here, or where I will go if I do leave. There was an order for me to leave here and return to the regiment when I am well, but I am beginning to think that from here we will go to some port and sail for the United States.…I have been on the front since I have been here, and didn't miss any of the fighting.*[177]

James Milton survived being gassed in France and returned home. After the Great War had ended, hundreds of veterans returned home from the front. Life seemed to return to a sense of normalcy. Charles Town has no monument to the First World War, but for a while, it had a living monument. A man by the name of Frank Buckles had moved to Charles Town sometime later. Buckles ended up being the last surviving member of the American Expeditionary Forces. When Frank was asked some years before his death about being the last surviving veteran of the First World War, he replied, "Someone has to do it."[178] That simple line can be said of the whole Jefferson County experience during the world war. The work was hard, grueling, mentally draining and at times emotional, but someone had to do it. The people of Jefferson County certainly did.

NOTES

Preface

1. American Battle Monuments Commission, "Meuse-Argonne American Cemetery."

Introduction

2. The claim for oldest town in West Virginia is only challenged by the town of Romney, West Virginia.
3. Leatherwood, "World War I."
4. Keys, *Historic Jefferson County*, 534–40; *Shepherdstown Register*, "Honor Roll"; Gozdzik, "Historic Resource Study," 122.

Chapter 1

5. National Park Service, "Casualties of Battle."
6. *Shepherdstown Register*, "War."
7. Ibid., "War in Europe."
8. Ibid., "Statement from the President."
9. Ibid., "Peace Meeting in Shepherdstown."
10. Ware, "Letter from Paris."
11. *Shepherdstown Register*, "From the Scene of War."

12. Ware, "Paris in War-Time."
13. Irwin, "Uncle Sam Offers All Americans."
14. *Shepherdstown Register*, "Terrible Crime."
15. *Shepherd Picket*, "Rumsey Memorial."
16. Cornwell, "Letter from Governor Cornwell."
17. *Shepherdstown Register*, "Notes of Our Soldiers," April 18, 1918.
18. Ibid., "How to Make Potato War Bread."
19. Ibid., "Potato Doughnuts."
20. Horn, "Community."
21. *Shepherdstown Register*, "Pershing's Crusaders."
22. Ibid., "Buy a Liberty Bond."
23. Ibid., "Over the Top."
24. Ibid., "Liberty Day in Shepherdstown."
25. Waldeck, "Proclamation by the Mayor of Shepherdstown."
26. *Shepherdstown Register*, "Notes of Our Soldiers," April 18, 1918.
27. Ibid., "Local Happenings."
28. Ibid., "C. and O. Canal."
29. Riddle, "Annual Report."
30. *Shepherdstown Register*, "Splendid Work of the Red Cross."
31. Ibid., "Efforts of the Red Cross."
32. Ibid., "Red Cross Report."
33. Ibid., "Report of the Jefferson County Chapter."
34. Ibid., "Red Cross at the Horse Show," August 1, 1918.
35. Ibid., "Appreciation of the Red Cross."
36. Ibid., "Letters of Appreciation."
37. Ibid., "Letters from Our Soldier Boys."
38. Ibid., "Letters from Our Boys in the Service."
39. Ibid., "Letters from Lieutenant Osbourn."
40. Ibid., "Another Letter from Lieut. Osbourn."
41. Ibid., "Notes of Our Soldiers," August 1, 1918.
42. Ibid. August 8, 1918.
43. Ibid., September 26, 1918.
44. Ibid., January 24, 1918.
45. Ibid., "A Letter from Corporal Shipley."
46. Ibid., "Corporal Shipley Writes Home."
47. Ibid., "Notes of Our Soldiers," August 8, 1918.
48. Ibid., "Where They Fall the Thickest."
49. Ibid., "News from Our Soldier Boys," March 7, 1918.
50. Ibid., "Notes of Our Soldiers," March 14, 1918.

51. Ibid., "Letter from Sergeant Snyder."
52. Snyder, "When the War Ended."
53. *Shepherd Picket*, "All Honor to Our Soldier Dead," March 1919.

Chapter 2

54. Today, the college is called Shepherd University, the name change having been approved in 2004 via legislation signed by Governor Bob Wise.
55. Horn, "College."
56. Ibid.
57. Ibid.
58. *Shepherd Picket*, "Editorial."
59. Ibid., "Shepherd College Dormitory."
60. Ibid., "Preparedness."
61. Young Men's Christian Association, "Two Calls."
62. *Shepherd Picket*, "To Those Who Left Us."
63. Ibid., "Christian Associations."
64. Ibid., "We Fight for Alsace-Lorraine."
65. *Shepherdstown Register*, "Honor Roll."
66. *Shepherd Picket*, "Our Soldier and Sailor Boys."
67. Ibid., "Alumni News."
68. *Shepherdstown Register*, "Word from France."
69. *Shepherd Picket*, "Letters from Our Boys."
70. Ibid.
71. Ibid., "Experiences in the Army and Navy."
72. Ibid., "Records of Soldiers."
73. Ibid., "More Soldier Records."
74. Ibid.
75. Barbe, "Stars of Gold."
76. *Shepherd Picket*, "All Honor to Our Soldier Dead," May–June 1919.
77. Ibid.
78. Ibid.
79. Ibid.
80. Ibid.
81. Ibid.
82. Ibid.
83. Ibid., "In Honor of Our Heroes."

Chapter 3

84. Harpers Ferry National Historical Park, "Post–Civil War Resource Study," 39–45.
85. Ibid., 45.
86. *Shepherdstown Register*, "Hill Top House."
87. Harpers Ferry National Historical Park, "Post–Civil War Resource Study," 46.
88. Ibid., 47.
89. Ibid., "Visiting Jefferson Rock."
90. Flanagan, "Reflection! Harpers Ferry," 15.
91. Ibid., 16.
92. *Shepherdstown Register*, "Training Our Men in Service."
93. Ibid., "Death Record."
94. Ibid., "News from Our Soldier Boys," April 25, 1918.
95. Ibid., "Notes of Our Soldiers," June 6, 1918.
96. Ibid., June 18, 1918.
97. Ibid., September 29, 1918.
98. *Harpers Ferry (WV) Storer Record*, "Letters from Over There and Elsewhere."
99. American Battle Monuments Commission, "Clarence C. Grove."
100. *Shepherdstown Register*, "Death Calls to Many."
101. *Shepherd Picket*, "We Mourn the Loss of Professor Duke."

Chapter 4

102. *Shepherdstown Register*, "Supreme Court."
103. Barbeau and Florette, *Unknown Soldiers*, 7.
104. Keene, "Great War in the African American Community," 61.
105. Barbeau and Florette, *Unknown Soldiers*, 11.
106. Ibid., 34.
107. Ibid., 43–44.
108. Keys, *Historic Jefferson County*, 534–40.
109. Gilmore, *Defying Dixie*, 17.
110. *Shepherdstown Register*, "Opera House."
111. Ibid., "Birth of a Nation Wednesday."
112. Ibid., "Notes of Our Soldiers," January 10, 1918.
113. Ibid., "Jefferson County Sends 61 More."
114. Ibid., "Colored Contingent All Right."

115. Ibid., "Notes of Our Soldiers," August 8, 1918.
116. Ibid., "Notes on Our Soldiers."
117. Ibid., "Notes of Our Soldiers," April 11, 1918.
118. Ibid., September 26, 1918.
119. American Battle Monuments Commission, "Martin Snyder."
120. Gozdzik, "Historic Resource Study," 122.
121. *Harpers Ferry (WV) Storer Record*, "Helmets."
122. Ibid., "War Souvenirs."
123. Ibid., "Helmets."
124. Ibid., "War Souvenirs."
125. Ibid., "Helmets."
126. Ibid., "Letters from Over There and Elsewhere."
127. Ibid., "Helmets."
128. Ibid.
129. Ibid., "Letters from Over There and Elsewhere."
130. Ibid.
131. Ibid.
132. Ibid.
133. Keene, "Great War in the African American Community," 61.
134. *Harpers Ferry (WV) Storer Record*, "News from Soldier Boys."
135. Ibid., "Letters from Over There and Elsewhere."
136. Ibid.
137. American Battle Monuments Commission, "John W. Tindley."
138. Gilmore, *Defying Dixie*, 18.
139. Barbeau and Florette, *Unknown Soldiers*, 177.
140. Ibid.
141. Ibid., 178.
142. Ibid., 176.
143. Ibid., 178.
144. Ibid., 181.
145. Gilmore, *Defying Dixie*, 18.
146. Barbeau and Florette, *Unknown Soldiers*, 181.
147. Ibid., 184–85.
148. Ibid., 187.
149. Ibid., 186.
150. Gozdzik, "Historic Resource Study," 125.
151. *Harpers Ferry (WV) Storer Record*, "Letters from Over There and Elsewhere."

Chapter 5

152. Perks, "History in Brief."
153. One raider was not found guilty of treason due to the fact that he was African American—the Dred Scott Supreme Court decision stated that African Americans were not citizens, thus he could not be found guilty of treason. He was, however, found guilty of the other two crimes.
154. Perks, "History in Brief."
155. *Shepherdstown Register*, "Field Artillery."
156. Ibid., "Life in the Trenches."
157. Ibid., "New Explosive Kills by Asphyxiation."
158. Ibid., "German Machine."
159. Ibid., "Fearful Losses in the European War."
160. Ibid., "If the Draft Bill Becomes Law."
161. Ibid., "West Virginia Preparing for the War."
162. Ibid., "Draft Board."
163. Ibid., "Shepherdstown Not Represented on the Board."
164. Ibid., "Form of Army Draft Registration Blank."
165. Ibid., "Class 1 Men to Fight."
166. Ibid., "News of Our Soldiers," January 10, 1918.
167. Ibid., "Notes on Soldiers."
168. Ibid., "Classification of Registrations."
169. Ibid., "Draft and Enrollment."
170. Ibid., "News of Our Soldiers," February 7, 1918.
171. Ibid., "Jefferson County Sends 61 More."
172. Ibid., "News of Our Soldiers," January 10, 1918.
173. Ibid., "News from Our Soldier Boys," May 16, 1918.
174. Ibid., "Notes of Our Soldiers," July 25, 1918.
175. Ibid., August 8, 1918.
176. Ibid., September 5, 1918.
177. Milton, "Letter to John Milton."
178. Rubin, *Last of the Doughboys*, 475.

BIBLIOGRAPHY

American Battle Monuments Commission. "Clarence C. Grove." November 14, 2016. https://www.abmc.gov/node/332654#.WCoaVvorLIU.

———. "John W. Tindley." November 14, 2016. https://www.abmc.gov/node/344388#.WCq2GPorLIU.

———. "Martin Snyder." November 14, 2016. https://www.abmc.gov/node/351331#.WCplV_orLIU.

———. "Meuse-Argonne American Cemetery." https://www.abmc.gov/cemeteries-memorials/europe/meuse-argonne-american-cemetery.

Barbe, Waitman. "Stars of Gold." *Shepherd Picket*, May–June 1919.

Barbeau, Arthur E., and Henri Florette. *The Unknown Soldiers: Black American Troops in World War I*. Philadelphia, PA: Temple University Press, 1974.

Cornwell, John J. "Letter from Governor Cornwell." *Shepherdstown Register*, April 12, 1917.

Flanagan, Isabel Kern. "Reflection! Harpers Ferry—When the Twentieth Century Was Young." Scrapbook, Harpers Ferry, West Virginia.

Gilmore, Glenda Elizabeth. *Defying Dixie: The Radical Roots of Civil Rights, 1919–1950*. New York: W.W. Norton, 2009.

Gozdzik, Gloria. "A Historic Resource Study for Storer College." Historic Resource Study, Harpers Ferry, West Virginia, 2002.

Harpers Ferry National Historical Park. "Post–Civil War Resource Study." National Park Service, Department of the Interior.

———. "Visiting Jefferson Rock." November 14, 2016. https://www.nps.gov/hafe/learn/historyculture/jefferson-rock.htm.

Harpers Ferry (WV) Storer Record. "Helmets." March 1919.

———. "Letters from Over There and Elsewhere." March 1919.

———. "News from Soldier Boys." May 1919.

———. "War Souvenirs." May 1919.

Horn, James. "The College." Century America Project, April 2014. http://shepherd.centuryamerica.org/the-college.

———. "The Community." Century America Project, April 2014. shepherd.centuryarmerica.org.

Irwin, Will. "Uncle Sam Offers All Americans a Chance to Feed Starving Belgium." *Shepherdstown Register*, January 7, 1915.

Keene, Jennifer D. "The Great War in the African American Community." In *Unknown Soldiers: The American Expeditionary Forces in Memory and Remembrance.* Edited by Mark A. Snell. Kent, OH: Kent State University Press, 2008.

Keys, Lesley F. *Historic Jefferson County.* Charles Town, WV: Jefferson County Historic Preservation and Archives, 1992.

Leatherwood, Jeffery M. "World War I." West Virginia Encyclopedia, September 30, 2015. http://www.wvencyclopedia.org/articles/1351.

Milton, James. "Letter to John Milton." Letter, France, 1918.

National Park Service. "Casualties of Battle." October 31, 2016. https://www.nps.gov/anti/learn/historyculture/casualties.htm.

Perks, Doug. "History in Brief." City of Charles Town, WV, November 15, 2016. http://www.charlestownwv.us/index.asp?Type=B_BASIC&SEC=%7B34C2969E-6CBC-4119-8C59-B78A2D0EBB77%7D.

Riddle, Katharine W. "Annual Report of the Jefferson County Chapter of the Red Cross." *Shepherdstown Register*, December 12, 1918.

Rubin, Richard. *The Last of the Doughboys.* New York: Houghton Mifflin Harcourt Publishing Company, 2013.

Shepherd Picket. "All Honor to Our Soldier Dead." March 1919.

———. "All Honor to Our Soldier Dead." May–June 1919.

———. "Alumni News." October—November 1917.

———. "Christian Associations." October–November 1917.

———. "Editorial." December 1919.

———. "Experiences in the Army and Navy." May 1919.

———. "In Honor of Our Heroes." March 1919.

———. "Letters from Our Boys." May–June 1918.

———. "More Soldier Records." July 1919.

———. "Our Soldier and Sailor Boys." March 1919.

———. "Preparedness." March 1916.

———. "Records of Soldiers." May 1919.
———. "The Rumsey Memorial." June–July 1915.
———. "Shepherd College Dormitory." January 1916.
———. "To Those Who Left Us." May–June 1917.
———. "We Fight for Alsace-Lorraine." May–June 1918.
———. "We Mourn the Loss of Professor Duke." March 1919.
Shepherdstown (WV) Register. "Another Letter from Lieut. Osbourn." July 4, 1918.
———. "Appreciation of the Red Cross." January 17, 1918.
———. "Birth of a Nation Wednesday." January 3, 1918.
———. "Buy a Liberty Bond." May 24, 1917.
———. "The C. and O. Canal." September 26, 1918.
———. "Classification of Registrations." January 24, 1918.
———. "Class 1 Men to Fight." January 10, 1918.
———. "Colored Contingent All Right." July 11, 1918.
———. "Corporal Shipley Writes Home." June 27, 1918.
———. "Death Calls to Many." October 17, 1918.
———. "The Death Record." February 14, 1918.
———. "The Draft and Enrollment." January 10, 1918.
———. "The Draft Board." May 24, 1917.
———. "Efforts of the Red Cross." May 2, 1918.
———. "Fearful Losses in the European War." April 22, 1915.
———. "Field Artillery." September 17, 1914.
———. "Form of Army Draft Registration Blank." May 24, 1917.
———. "From the Scene of War." September 17, 1914.
———. "The German Machine." February 4, 1915.
———. "Hill Top House." August 13, 1914.
———. "Honor Roll." May 1919.
———. "How to Make Potato War Bread." February 7, 1918.
———. "If the Draft Bill Becomes Law." April 26, 1917.
———. "Jefferson County Sends 61 More." June 27, 1918.
———. "A Letter from Corporal Shipley." April 4, 1918.
———. "Letter from Sergeant Snyder." August 22, 1918.
———. "Letters from Lieutenant Osbourn." June 27, 1918.
———. "Letters from Our Boys in the Service." April 25, 1918.
———. "Letters from Our Soldier Boys." April 18, 1918.
———. "Letters of Appreciation." April 4, 1918.
———. "Liberty Day in Shepherdstown." April 25, 1918.
———. "Life in the Trenches." December 17, 1914.

———. "Local Happenings." May 3, 1917.
———. "New Explosive Kills by Asphyxiation." July 8, 1915.
———. "News from Our Soldier Boys." April 25, 1918.
———. "News from Our Soldier Boys." March 7, 1918.
———. "News from Our Soldier Boys." May 16, 1918.
———. "News of Our Soldiers." February 7, 1918.
———. "News of Our Soldiers." January 24, 1918.
———. "Notes of Our Soldiers." April 18, 1918.
———. "Notes of Our Soldiers." April 11, 1918.
———. "Notes of Our Soldiers." August 8, 1918.
———. "Notes of Our Soldiers." August 1, 1918.
———. "Notes of Our Soldiers." January 10, 1918.
———. "Notes of Our Soldiers." June 18, 1918.
———. "Notes of Our Soldiers." June 6, 1918.
———. "Notes of Our Soldiers." March 14, 1918.
———. "Notes of Our Soldiers." September 5, 1918.
———. "Notes of Our Soldiers." September 29, 1918.
———. "Notes of Our Soldiers." September 26, 1918.
———. "Notes on Our Soldiers." July 25, 1918.
———. "Notes on Soldiers." January 17, 1918.
———. "Opera House." January 3, 1918.
———. "Over the Top." April 25, 1918.
———. "Peace Meeting in Shepherdstown." October 8, 1914.
———. "Pershing's Crusaders." July 25, 1918.
———. "Potato Doughnuts." February 7, 1918.
———. "Red Cross at the Horse Show." August 1, 1918.
———. "Red Cross Report." May 9, 1918.
———. "Report of the Jefferson County Chapter American Red Cross." September 12, 1918.
———. "Shepherdstown Not Represented on the Board." May 24, 1917.
———. "Splendid Work of the Red Cross." January 3, 1918.
———. "Statement from the President." August 20, 1914.
———. "The Supreme Court." June 24, 1915.
———. "A Terrible Crime." May 13, 1915.
———. "Training Our Men in Service." January 10, 1918.
———. "War." August 6, 1914.
———. "The War in Europe." August 20, 2914.
———. "West Virginia Preparing for the War." May 3, 1917.
———. "Where They Fall the Thickest." October 31, 1918.

———. "Word from France." January 3, 1918.

Snyder, William. "When the War Ended." *Shepherdstown Register*, December 5, 1918.

Waldeck, J.L. "A Proclamation by the Mayor of Shepherdstown, W. VA." *Shepherdstown Register*, April 25, 1918.

Ware, John. "A Letter from Paris." *Shepherdstown Register*, August 27, 1914.

———. "Paris in War-Time." *Shepherdstown Register*, September 24, 1914.

Young Men's Christian Association. "The Two Calls." *Shepherd Picket*, March 1916.

ABOUT THE AUTHOR

James Francis Horn is from Marriottsville in Carroll County, Maryland. Upon graduating from South Carroll High School in 2010, Horn attended Shepherd University. While at Shepherd, Horn became a brother of the Lambda Chi Alpha fraternity. He also was president of Phi Alpha Theta, the national history honors society, for a semester. In 2012, James began volunteering at Antietam National Battlefield. In 2013, Horn was a living history intern at Harpers Ferry National Historical Park. In his senior year, Horn served as a Teagle Foundation scholar for the Council of Public Liberal Arts Colleges (COPLAC), working on the Century America Project. James graduated from Shepherd University in May 2014 with a degree in history, with a concentration in the Civil War and nineteenth-century America. Upon graduation, Horn began employment as a seasonal park ranger at Harpers Ferry National Historical Park. Currently, Horn is a seasonal park ranger at Cedar Creek and Belle Grove National Historical Park in Middletown, Virginia.